MARKET DOMINATION FOR PODCASTING

"Seth, at the racetrack I say, it's luck when you lose, skill and cunning you when you win. You do not need luck. Seth Greene's data mining of live time credit card purchase data of other people's customers is exceptional.

Dan Kennedy, a serial, successful, multi-millionaire entrepreneur; trusted marketing advisor, consultant and coach to hundreds of private entrepreneurial clients running businesses from $1-million to $1-billion in size. For over 30+ years he has created winning campaigns for health, diet and beauty products and companies, B2B and industry products including software, and investments. and other publications.

Dave Dee is one of Dan Kennedy's most successful students. Dave saw Dan speak over 15 years ago at one of the Peter Lowe Success Events when he was a struggling magician. He bought Magnetic Marketing and as you will hear when he tells you his story, his life changed in less than 90 days. Dave became a very serious student of Dan's by attending my seminars, joining his coaching group and most of all from implementing what he learned. Dave has become a top flight mentor and expert and is the GKIC Chief Marketing Officer.

"We've got Seth Greene and that's very important."

"We've talked and I'm a potential and future customer of what you're doing right now. I think it's really cool and I want to be a part of it.I remember when you first explained it to me and I understood what it was, it blew my mind that something like that is even possible. That's what your magic is!"

—Russell Brunson

"We highly recommend Seth and his firm without reservation. Hire him. You will not regret it."

—Dr. Dustin Burlseon, DDS

"Seth is his one of the smartest marketers on the planet. He's been Nominated Back-To-Back by Dan Kennedy for Marketer of the Year (never been done before), runs my personal marketing campaigns and is the most honest and reputable person I know.

If you want your marketing and/or businesses to go to the next level, hire him. Don't question it, just do it.

When I need help with marketing I hire him. Period.

—Graig Presti, CEO – Local Search

"I came away very impressed with his timely response and his dedication to "getting 'er done". You have a keeper in Seth."

—Thomas J. Fogerty, CFP, The Pinnacle Planning Group, LLC

Seth Greene is amazing. He has been offering his time to help me pull together some marketing strategies, and his suggestions are great, his advice is sound, and I really feel total support from him to move forward in my practice. I am really grateful for all he is sharing with me to grow my business — it's making a big difference for me.

—Arpana

"I just wanted you to know how much I have enjoyed working with Seth on my coaching. He has been very helpful and his knowledge level is exceptional."

—**Barton Close**, Classic Wealth Advisory

"I look forward to working with them to help build my business. They did a great job in attracting me to their service. I am going to implement targeting my clients better and use differentiation strategies right away. These strategies are brilliant. I cannot wait to tell my group about some of the ideas."

—**Kris Hart**, Morgan Stanley, Worcester, MA

"You brought many great and creative ideas in a simple and straight forward manner. was interested in every minute of what you were talking about. I was very impressed by the explanation and theory behind each marketing objective. I am looking forward to next month and hope to have implemented two ideas that were discussed."

—**Jeff Layhew**, Liverpoool, NY

"Boring letters and seminars don't work. This is a great program … works great in building up a client base"

—**Stephanie Tyler**, Merrill Lynch.

"I like that the ideas do not require you to take a second job as the marketing director for your practice gets me in front of more ideal clients and referrals."

—**George Cox**, Merrill Lynch

"…inspiring and very motivational. I see this program benefiting my practice in more ways that I can even begin to articulate! I love having the ability to leave 800 voicemails in a matter of seconds. The handwritten postcards that can be sent via computer are great"

—**Ryan Crowley**, Morgan Stanley

"I see this program increasing the number of ideal clients I work with. It touches my clients more by automating the marketing process."

—**Ian Clarke-Pounder**, Morgan Stanley

"I switched to Market Domination from my previous marketing coach. Seth brought together marketing & contact ideas with a strategy that looks to be both effective and efficient. Market Domination will enable me to be more visible, and to have a better relationship with my clients. I am going to start with a newsletter, auto phone contact, and letters & postcards."

—**Mark Procknal**, LPL Financial

"I couldn't make notes fast enough. I am very impressed. I get good ideas; they don't cost a lot of money – in fact they should save me money vs. what I am doing now.

I used your "Doctor Close" at one of my seminars. I held two seminars the same week. We had 28 people at both seminars (28 was the maximum seating). At the first seminar I presented the way I always do, and I set one appointment from that group. Well, one appointment isn't going to cut it. I spent too much money and too much of my time for such a poor result.

At the second seminar two days later. I used the doctor close, and really embellished this time. I then let the attendees give me feedback. It got them participating I think it really made them think. I then finished with the rest of the "Doctor close". I increased my appointment close ratio over 900% that night! Much, much better results. Thanks Seth for coming through again."

—**Gary Alden**, Kingwood, Texas

"After using the automated call process that Seth recommends, I had 2 clients call within 15 minutes ready to discuss options for their portfolio. Our lives will definitely be easier using this technology, Thanks, Seth for the tip…"

—**Jeff Peters**

The Summit Brokerage Success Story: "I wanted to let you know how well your ATM Technology worked for me. I don't know why I didn't do it sooner. Initially, I was hesitant not knowing what to expect. However I took the "plunge" last week for the first time.

My first call campaign was to almost 1200 numbers scheduled for after office hours at approximately 7:30 PM on a Thursday. Within 1 minute of the scheduled call campaign, I started receiving phone calls, one after the other. This went on for about an hour. I could not keep up with it.

The next day, the first call came in at 6:00 AM! And by 8:15 AM, the phone just rang constantly. It was hard to hear the person I was talking to due to the distraction from the call waiting beeps! This continued throughout the day with the last call coming at 6:15 PM.

Of this call campaign, there were 60 human answers and 940 voicemail messages left. I received approximately 65 calls in total, of which 5 were candidates that were "ready" for what I had to offer. Another 12 seemed very interested who asked for an informational package with a follow up call the following week. 6.9% of my prospects Called Me! I am very excited!

All in all, I think what I learned from this "experiment, aside from knowing that it works, it to NOT send that many messages at once. It was too much to keep up with at the level of professional service that I want to give. So since that first campaign, I have done one more with a manageable number of 300. There were 240 voicemails left, and I have received 16 phone calls today.

Needless, to say these folks got my undivided attention and it looks like there is some good opportunity for more business. Seth, thank you so much for turning me on to this wonderful marketing advantage!!"

—**Kathleen F,** Summit Brokerage

"I purchased a subscription to the Market Domination Program in 2011 and began using the newsletters and monthly marketing ideas. My compliance department ran into some issues with some of the marketing pieces, but most specifically the flag-ship 7 deadly mistakes piece. We went back and forth with them, with assistance from Seth, but ultimately they decided that they were not going to approve it. So I begrudgingly went to the Market Domination Program to ask for a full refund since the #1 piece that I wanted to use was not getting approved. And without any hesitation or argument, they refunded my money. Although I didn't really get a chance to use the main flagship marketing piece and can't speak to its success, I can speak to the fact that if things don't work out for you in you're back office approval process, this company's guarantee is rock solid in my opinion."

—Jeff B.

BEFORE YOU GET STARTED…
Make sure to subscribe, rate and review my
Direct Response Marketing Podcast please!
https://ultimatemarketingmagician.com/podcasts

Amazing Free Offer!

Register to attend a LIVE training webinar with me (Seth Greene), where I walk you through the same step-by-step process we use to get great results for our podcast and the podcast's of our clients.

You will Learn:

- How to Double Your Referrals with a Podcast!
- How to Get 20 Referral Partners Promoting Your Business in 20 Minutes A Week!
- How to Get Impossible To Reach Decision Makers To Seek You Out!

Go here to sign up, it's free:
http://www.ultimatemarketingmagician.com/pmmwebinar

MARKET DOMINATION
FOR PODCASTING

Secrets From the World's Top Podcasters

SETH GREENE

New York

MARKET DOMINATION FOR PODCASTING
Secrets From the World's Top Podcasters

Published in New York, New York, by Morgan James Publishing. Morgan James and The Entrepreneurial Publisher are trademarks of Morgan James, LLC. www.MorganJamesPublishing.com

The Morgan James Speakers Group can bring authors to your live event. For more information or to book an event visit The Morgan James Speakers Group at www.TheMorganJamesSpeakersGroup.com.

Shelfie

A **free** eBook edition is available
with the purchase of this print book.

ISBN 978-1-63047-925-1 paperback
ISBN 978-1-63047-996-1 eBook
Library of Congress Control Number:
2016903706

Cover Design by:
Chris Treccani
www.3dogdesign.net

Interior Design by:
Bonnie Bushman
The Whole Caboodle Graphic Design

CLEARLY PRINT YOUR NAME ABOVE IN UPPER CASE

Instructions to claim your free eBook edition:
1. Download the Shelfie app for Android or iOS
2. Write your name in **UPPER CASE** above
3. Use the Shelfie app to submit a photo
4. Download your eBook to any device

In an effort to support local communities, raise awareness and funds, Morgan James Publishing donates a percentage of all book sales for the life of each book to Habitat for Humanity Peninsula and Greater Williamsburg.
Get involved today! Visit
www.MorganJamesBuilds.com

DEDICATION

To my amazing wife Rebecca, who puts up with my entrepreneurial mood swings, shiny object syndrome, and all the other fun parts of being married to a serial entrepreneur.

To my wonderful children, Max, Ella, and Lillie – who keep me young and energetic.

To my awesome team members, who make me look good and get great results for our wonderful clients.

To the amazing entrepreneurs who agreed to be in this book – I couldn't have done it without you!

And as always, to the legendary Dan Kennedy, without whom none of this would be possible.

TABLE OF CONTENTS

Podcast Mastermind!

Bonus Marketing Interviews

INTRODUCTION

Before we learn from some amazing Podcasters, I want to spill the beans ahead of time, and share with you our secret sauce.

The point of having a Podcast is not to have a podcast.

Here are the points of having a Podcast:

1. With a Podcast you have a media platform. That means you are, in essence a reporter. Being a reporter who owns a media platform can get you access (as we will show you in later chapters) to people you otherwise couldn't get to, and places you couldn't otherwise go (can you say press pass?)

2. You are no longer chasing prospects or decision makers. You are now the person they seek out, as you have what everyone else wants – the ability to grant exposure (every business owner, thought leader, etc. wants more exposure).

3. You have something to promote every single week – your latest podcast episode.

4. You have a platform for repurposing content. Every episode of your podcast should be transcribed, edited, and turned into a chapter in your next book. That way you write a book without writing a book.

5. Guess who will promote your podcast? Everyone who appears on an episode! They were on it, so of course they will tell their email list and social media followers about it. Podcasting is a great way to get access to other people's lists – or build a list if you don't have one (or grow it really fast).

6. Guess who will promote your book? Everyone who is in it (your podcast guests)! So not only do they promote your podcast when their episode airs, but when the book comes out with them in it – they promote you all over again. It's a great way to create essentially an army of high level affiliates!

7. Let's take the example of one of our Done For You Podcasting clients, a financial advisor. If he asks an estate planning attorney to hand out his business card to all of the attorney's clients, that attorney will throw him out of his office. If our financial advisor puts the attorney on his podcast, and then in his book – our attorney will buy 200 copies of the book he is in, and happily hand them out to all his clients! Do you see how magical that is?

Now that you know what the end game is, let's dive right in and see how some of the top Podcaster's in the world work their magic...

INTERVIEW WITH
KARL KRUMMENACHER

Seth: Today I have the good fortune of interviewing Karl Krummenacher of Wellness Media Group. Karl, welcome to the show.

Karl: Seth, it's great to be here today.

Seth: Thank you so much. Can you tell our listeners a little bit about how you got started?

Karl: I've been a lifelong entrepreneur. In December of last year, I actually decided to step back from a busy job as a president of a direct sales company specializing in making personalized nutrition and skin care based on DNA. It's a cool company. After working on that for three years, I started to ask some questions about what I really wanted to do and focus on – I've been a fan of direct response marketing for years. I loved the health and wellness space.

I used direct response to grow my network marketing business and generate product sales for myself, my team and clients. After growing a large team I started to find ways to apply direct response strategies throughout my career after that.

Back in December of last year, I made the decision to apply all that I learned in health and wellness along with direct response marketing to help consumers and health care professionals find each other. The idea was to create a platform of platforms. Something that would really transcend any personality and allow consumers to gain access to the wealth of incredible information that exists today about living a truly happy and healthy life.

You know Seth, when we are born; our bodies are one of the most complex systems on the planet. The problem is that there's no manual. Over the last 100 years or so, technology and medicines evolved, but the practice of wellness was going the other way.

People are getting many times the healthcare interactions they got just 20 years ago, but the outcomes are worse. The generation born in the last five years is expected to be the first to live a shorter life span than the ones that preceded them.

I've been exposed to several experts in health, nutrition, personal development, the psychology of happiness. Many of the experts I've met or interviewed have remarkable evidence-based research and have discovered really cool things about measurably changing health outcomes. But for any number of reasons, they're not getting the attention of mainstream media. So that became my goal – to get around this organizing principle that transcends any personality which is wellness and create a platform of platforms, leveraging the reach of our existing list of subscribers and develop a syndicate of content that helps people that we're calling the Wellness Radio Network.

That's why I formed the company Wellness Media Group. We want to invest in businesses and people focused on delivering consumers true wellness. Initially we made an investment in wellness.com - they get it, and as a company are working hard to surface the best, most actionable content available for consumers to get the greatest results with the least effort.

Next we created a new media property, the Your Best Life Podcast, which just opened three weeks ago. And in that period of time, we've been fortunate to get just over 24,000 downloads for the first 21 days, make it to number two, in New and Noteworthy on iTunes and do some dramatic list building for the experts that we featured.

Seth: That's incredible. How have you grown so fast?

Karl: Practicing the principles that I've been exposed to by some of the greats, people like Dan Kennedy, Ryan Deiss, Perry Belcher. These guys had a dramatic influence on how I thought about marketing. We basically took all of the wellness related information that we have access to and looked at the way that we could leverage that across multiple platforms. And when I speak of a platform, what I mean by that is an expert's or an author's tribe, or existing list.

So the strategy was kind of simple. Wellness.com is a great brand. It is the brand of wellness. Because of the hard work of its founders it generates over a 100,000 unique visitors every day from a long tail search. So, if you were to search cardiologist in San Diego or your physician's name, there's better chance than not a wellness.com directory entry for the physician, procedure or practice type will show up in the first page you Google.

That's generated traffic which was monetized with Google ad sales revenue. Until last year there was no focused list building going on. The first thing my partners at wellness. com did was start building and warming their list so that they could 'on-demand' reach people who expressed an interest in who we were.

Next, we decided if we're going to publish great content we have two choices, we could either be the author or we could be the publisher. That's something I learned from Ryan Deiss. It's so powerful. We're not the experts. We are really publishers. We can publish, edit and organize the information provided by leading experts. That's the right way to approach this market. We didn't need to be the expert. In fact, it would be impossible to be credible experts in all the various areas of health and wellness.

Shortly after we made that decision I started making phone calls. I discovered a great company run by Jessica Rhodes, called Interview Connections, a division of Entrepreneur Support Systems. Jessica has a cool service for podcasters which will reach out and secure great guests. I made a list of the people I knew that had evidence-based research with credible outcomes, people that were really moving the needle in the health and wellness space in their particular niche or category and who had or could develop a following.

I was surprised by how simple it is to get people to engage. Because like any other direct marketer, regardless if they did it for 10 years and they have millions of people following them or they're just getting started, everyone needs exposure to the right audience. These experts, if they're in tune with what it takes to get their message out, know the principles that will help create engagement and build their business and their brand.

This meant most were very open and willing to be on our podcast. Since I wasn't an expert at podcasting, I searched for what's available to learn how to do this right and found a course called Podcasters Paradise by John Lee Dumas. I jumped in to that, consumed as quickly as I could and followed those steps to a "T" to make sure that I focused on the essential few things that I needed to do in order to get the podcast launched quickly to a wide audience, and to get other people to promote it and start to build a new syndicate around wellness. I think those were the key things that we did that have the biggest difference.

Seth: I met Jessica at an event. She does a great job. You're absolutely right. And let me ask you this, what do you wish you knew when you started that you know now?

Karl: Wow. Well, several things. That list is longer than the list of things that I already know for sure. First of all, I think people need to understand if you're going to build a podcast, solid production quality with an engaging host and interesting content is equally important to your core message.

I see a lot of people who are getting into podcasting who participate in Facebook groups that get all worked up about their logo, or all bent out of shape about what microphone to use – but they're not really investing any time listening to successful podcasts understanding how to engage a guest or how to deliver true value in audio content.

I wish I knew what the ideal show flow for a podcast like ours was before I started. What was really working? John Dumas's course covers how to do an interview but there are subtle pieces in my niche that, had I invested the time learning before I launched it could have been better. I would also have learned the ways that I could quickly systematize the work that goes in to generating a podcast.

Knowing for example the best outsourcing resources that can do the tech stuff for us more efficiently that we can so I could have spent more time focusing on prepping and really getting to know my guest.

I also wish I knew the impact that preparing my guest before the show would have on the actual show product. The most important thing that I've done to produce better shows is focus on truly engaging my guests before we actually get start recording the show. Ideally, I want them to listen to the show, to understand the flow, to know what I'm going to be asking, and I want them to get prepared. Personally, I really also want to know how can I help them the best.

There's a good book out there called *Give And Take* by Adam Grant. I enjoyed reading this book. Its principles are really true for entrepreneurs. The key concept: it is through giving without the expectation of return that we ultimately get what we need. Really knowing full impact of that concept as we got started has been helpful because we've found that the more that we work to freely give benefit to the experts who have the content that compels an audience's attention, the more content we get that provides people massive transformational value, and that's a game changer for us.

Making sure that you know exactly what you can do to provide your guests clear value to promote the interview to their list, to create value for what they're trying to achieve and having them prepared so that the interview and the show that you create both provide great value to your audience. It's extremely synergistic. Today we have an email list that in the last year has grown from nothing to 1.2 million subscribers. We can mail to them daily. It's literally money on demand and we were now seeing that if we drop the iTunes podcast and let our listeners to jump on our email newsletter, leverage the email list to promote the podcast and to promote the experts who are promoting us, the multiplier effect of this is just insane and the leverage is dramatically greater than anything I imagined it could be, far greater than the typical "if you build it they will come" approach.

Seth: Absolutely. You are proving an incredible amount of value. I greatly appreciate it. I mean you are trying to literally create a key change in the world with the amazing work that you're doing. What is your biggest challenge?

Karl: I think the biggest challenge that we have right now is prioritizing our business strategy. Like most entrepreneurs, we have a long list of things we'd love to do, along with the people we'd love to interview and shows we would like to produce. But once we got going with this, we learned some really fascinating things. Everybody knows that podcasts are hot now. Soon, a podcast is going to be available in your car like FM radio is. ITunes and the Apple interface is making its way to the car, which will become a primary medium for consumers to get the exact content that they want to listen too. It's going to provide marketers an incredible opportunity to connect with their ideal audience.

And so right now, our focus is on prioritizing our activities so that we can grow predictably while continuing to deliver value and not overwhelm ourselves. We need to budget time to sharpen the saw and still capture the market share that we want.

For example, right now, we're trying to find talent much like Leo Laporte did when he created "This week in tech." It was really the Granddaddy to lot of these modern day podcast shows and networks. He was summarily let go of the tech TV network which was on cable when the owner of that network decided to cancel the show and fire a lot of the people that were there. He said, you know what, "I think the future is in podcasting," and he started just like you and I are doing right now, interviewing some of the big voices in technology. That's grown to a radio network that has I think some 20 or so shows, several guests, a dedicated production facility. It's like a CNN newsroom for tech news where they produce content 24/7.

We started with that in mind and created the Wellness Radio Network. The first show was Your Best Life. We have organic shows that are in development. We have a show planned to reach healthcare providers. We have over one million providers featured on our site. These providers need a way to market their services, to step out from the crowd to be able to share their unique gifts to patients who are looking for better outcomes while improving practice incomes.

And so, we're opportunity rich with the real need for us to be disciplined in our focus so that we don't outspend our capacity; deliver great value to consumers and really focus on keeping the brand value high because so many people start these things – podcasts, blogs, everything, with an economic mindset. That's good for short term result but when you really set the focus beyond yourself and ask "What can I do to provide great value to my audience?" you win and consumers win.

We see our role as supporting the experts and the authors, and others in the wellness space that have incredible information consumers need to get easy access to. That is our mission. It's what I'm irrationally passionate about. Wellness focused living has changed my life dramatically. So the big question is "how do we pair consumers and providers together? What can we do to bridge these two groups and create value for everyone?" Because it's in value creation that we are ultimately rewarded.

It all boils down to prioritizing and staying focused first on value creation because then your intrinsic brand value never goes away. You know, whether it's a podcast today, a blog post tomorrow, working on a newsletter or an eBook, these are only technologies. These will come and go. But by focusing on the fundamentals of creating brand value by connecting consumers with the specific solution they need (even if that's the third party), you can position yourself as the intermediary in that equation and do exceptionally well without having to be an expert yourself. To do that you're the manager and the arbitrator of that information.

Were so excited about what we're doing to bring this information to consumers and we're seeing such quick results that it's easy to get distracted by the revenue potential and to do things that might quickly monetize and lose sight of the big picture and not create that killer brand that we can create by being disciplined.

Seth: You mentioned the book *Give And Take*, would you be so kind as to recommend to our listeners two other books you read that it had some of the biggest impact on your work?

Karl: Well, probably for the marketing perspective, I'd have to go with Dr. Robert Cialdini's book, *Influence*. The idea of being able to identify the key seven triggers that cause people to do things that they might not otherwise do if they were making "rational, sane" decisions. That book had a tremendous impact on me.

I think one of the challenges we have is not letting that ADD kick in and staying focused on the things we need to do to be fully present, to give 100 % and stay in the moment and not suffer the tyranny of the urgency. We've all got our cellphones going off in our pockets constantly, text messages, twitter messages, Facebook messages, and we're hooked on the Dopamine that we get from that anticipation of what's the next cool thing. And it really brought me back to center when I read Tony Schwartz's book "The Power Of Full Engagement."

I'll throw in a third one there, which is, you know, we could talk marketing books all day long, the list is long and notable. But I think another great book is *The Grain Brain* by Dr Perlmutter. It caused me to think a little bit differently about how to stay sharp as I age. It's a remarkable amount of research that's gone into how grains are affecting diabetes and metabolic syndrome but equally important, how many brain disorders are now being considered type 3 diabetes and this whole notion of Alzheimer's, dementia and even Parkinson's disease being influenced heavily by the huge amount of grain and sugar we eat.

We, as entrepreneurs, we need to stay sharp and focused and healthy and alive. And make sure that we sharpen the saw so stay effective. We take on more work than everybody else takes. We are very, very passionate about what we want to do and too often, I see great entrepreneurs with incredible ability to leave their special mark burnout because they didn't take time to sharpen the saw.

So I could give you a long list Seth but, you know, those are a couple of that come to mind. Dan Kennedy has got so many great books. I must have at least 10 of these, *The Ultimate Sales Letter* was a great start for me, *No B.S. Sales Success* was another great book. When I was an entrepreneur and trying to make the shift, it was so important for me to really understand what it took to run an enterprise - *eMyth* was a key by Michael Gerber. So there you go.

Seth: All great books, absolutely, incredible interview. An immense amount of value, I've got pages of notes. I'm sure our listeners do as well. We will obviously send them all to wellness.com and to get your podcast as well. Thank you so much. It's been an honor and a privilege to get to spend some time with you. We greatly appreciate it.

Karl: Seth, the honor was mine. Look forward to catching up with you again sometime in the future.

INTERVIEW WITH
JOEL BOGGESS

Joel: The ReLaunch podcast just turned 10 months old just a few weeks ago as we are recording this. And gosh, we sailed past 500,000 total plays in that 10-month period of time. We are on fire, excited about that. And on our podcast, we interview and we pick the brains of some of today's most creative and most innovative thought leaders, authors, speakers and really uncovering some of the secrets to their success and also learning from their come-from-behind stories. They're very inspirational and it really means a lot to me to get that kind of feedback, those tweets and e-mail back from our listeners. So it's been a blast. The ReLaunch show really provides inspiring stories, fresh ideas and then of course practical steps for people going through their own ReLaunch. Gosh, we've all experienced numerous launches and relaunches in our lives. So it's very easy to relate with I should say.

Seth: And you've had come an incredible way in a very short period of time. How have you grown your base so fast?

Joel: You know, one of the things that we did, Seth, which I think really served us well is we created at the very beginning of the launch, before the launch, we created a launch team. When I talk about a launch team, basically it's a conference room full of people that knew us, that liked us, that trusted us and that believed in the ReLaunch message. And it was our launch team. We had about 80, somewhere between 80 and 90 people on our launch team. It was that team that helped to promote our show via social media, via the people that they knew, the people that were on their list.

And that actually catapulted us quickly to our first number one in the iTunes new and noteworthy system and then our second number one and our third number and so forth and so on. We actually ended up hitting number one in our categories repeatedly through the entire debut period which was an eight-week period on iTunes. Even after that period, the momentum continued and our audience actually grew about 12-fold from that very first full broadcast month. I think we had maybe 7000 downloads that first full month to our highest month so far which has been 93,000 for the month. That's about a 12- or 13-fold increase and we're really excited about that.

Seth: It's an incredible growth rate. I think it's a testament to the amazing stories that you are telling and sharing with your listeners. How do you select and find such amazing guests?

Joel: Great question. I appreciate you giving me the opportunity to talk about this. You know, I want to hear from people that are not afraid to be open and transparent about their come-from-behind victories and the people that have reached a certain pinnacle of success, people like Jack Canfield, for instance, the creator behind the *Chicken Soup for the Soul* book series and many, many other projects. People that have reached a certain level of success understand that it's okay to share your come-from-behind stories and your struggles and your failures. So I'm looking for people that are not afraid to just put the guard down and to share. I asked Jack actually. I interviewed him a couple of months ago on my show.

I said, "Jack, what was the most challenging part of your life? What's the most challenging season that you went through?" Gosh, Seth, within 30 seconds of our interview, he was telling me about his divorce and how it was such a blow to him on multiple levels and he had already reached a status where he was earning and making and worth multimillions of dollars. And that season of his life ended up taking pretty much everything, 25 million dollars from his net worth which basically made him start all over again. That happened a long time ago and Jack kind of laughs about it now or at least he laughed with me on my show a little bit. And he said that, "Well, you know, Joel, my wife got a good lawyer and I got to keep my job."

People share those stories. At this point, we're very fortunate that people are actually coming to us because they see the value, not just being on the show but telling their story and letting people get the inspiration from "gosh, if he did it or if she did it, I can do it too." I interviewed a lady the other day that is a multiple bestselling author and she at one point in time in her life was living in her car in a Wal-Mart parking lot as a single woman. She had found some courage and some gumption within herself to pull herself up, to firm her boot straps and to relaunch if you will her life, her career and the relationship that she had with herself and with others. She was able to catapult herself into a whole different better season in her life.

Seth: Since you are so good at getting folks to share things like that that inspire us let me flip the microphone and ask you, what do you wish you knew when you started that you know now?

Joel: What do I wish I knew when I started that I know now? Transparency is priceless and what I mean by that is to share who you really are, not who you think you should be or who you think that people will relate with but to share the real you. That includes exposing your blemishes, your pimples, your false starts and failed attempts and just letting people know. I tell you what, Seth; I still struggle with that as we all do because we're all people. We're all part of the same race, the human race and we're not perfect. I still struggle with sharing all parts of me even the private parts if you will because they're not always pretty but it is priceless to be able to do that. People like Jack and like Rachel, that was the woman that lived in her car in the Wal-Mart parking lot, they were able to realize the benefit in being totally transparent because that's what makes people able to relate with them and to maybe learn something from their experiences. I still struggle with it but, as we all are, getting better.

Seth: We are all works in progress. What has been your biggest mistake? And what did you learn from it?

Joel: Sure. My biggest mistake is to build it first and hope that they will come. You probably remember that line.

Seth: Yes, of course. From the *Field of Dreams* movie.

Joel: From the Kevin Costner movie, absolutely. If you build it, they will come. That may have been true at one point in time in business but it's no longer true. So learning how to do the reverse of that to make sure that they will come before you build it that is the secret sauce to being a successful entrepreneur today. Making sure they will come before you build it and putting your concept, if you will, before they will come and then to make those tweaks to build up those improvements. You got to prove your concept.

Unfortunately, what a lot of people do is they spend their time, their effort, their resources building this stadium, if you will; sticking with that analogy, and then it's empty. And it stays empty for a long, long time and that can be absolutely expensive on multiple, multiple levels. However, if you see that there's interest in it, you know what, people are lining up already. Then you start to build it out. That's how you prove the concept. And based on the feedback that you get from your early adapters, you know, the people that show up early, and then based on what they say, and then you can make whatever improvements, adjustments, renovations that are needed so you can continue to improve and attract more people that way. I mean, did I say that correctly?

Seth: Yes, absolutely. Now that you have obviously, hopefully learned that lesson – I think we all sometimes fall guilty of it. Even though we know it intellectually, we still sometimes fall in love with an idea and start building it before we sell it or before we market it.

Joel: There's no question.

Seth: You've achieved an incredible level of success not just with the podcast but with everything else. You're a serial entrepreneur. What's your biggest challenge now?

Joel: Sure. That's a great question. Biggest challenge now is probably to – we're going through a re-launch of our show so to speak just to make sure that we're making the correct adjustments and tweaks in our show and in our business so that we can serve more people and that we can build upon our own business. That's the challenge right now. We've been having a blast. We're almost 11 months old actually now and our one-year anniversary is coming up in a little more than a month. We want to celebrate that by making our show even more valuable, offering more meaningful game changing content and talking with the movers and shakers in the world of business and just respecting people's time. So you asked what the greatest challenge is. It's to make sure that we make the best and the most appropriate renovations and structural changes in our show and business so that we can help more people doing what we've experienced and learned to do over this time and that's been writing bestselling books. We know how to do that. That's been creating a number one podcast. We've learned how to do that.

Also to help people become known in their niche, Seth. One of the ways to do that other than those other two options, choices that I have just given you is to get yourself booked on television, real television, not paid programming or advertisement, infomercials and all that but to get yourself to be newsworthy and on TV. In the past, I don't know, three or four years, I've been on TV on the news about 100 times. That is publicity you cannot pay for. When the news anchor holds up your book and points and says, "This is the book to have." Then your information is flashed up on the screen. You can't buy that kind of publicity. I teach people how to do it. I probably should've said this first but during the 90s,

Seth, I spent pretty much the entire decade being behind the microphone doing traditional radio and also in front of the camera doing TV. And what that means is I know how that industry works and also know how the game is played. I know how to get on the set and I know how to help people get on the set so they can position themselves as the expert in whatever niche or field that they're in even if they don't have big-time connections with Oprah and Dr. Phil or if they don't have a large social media at present. That's just one of the ways that we're helping people become known. That way is to get that television exposure.

A lot of today's entrepreneurs are focusing a lot of their time on new media. When I say new media, I'm talking about podcasts like what we're doing right now and e-books and Facebook and Twitter and all that stuff. All that stuff is great. Absolutely. If you haven't adopted it yet- get into it now. However, a lot of people are ignoring the traditional media, TV, radio. Well, most people still get their information that way. Right or wrong, that's still where most people get their information. So what I've done is I've taken traditional media by getting on TV, radio, things of that nature and then worked to blend it in with today's new media. So you're actually creating a marriage, a marriage that works between the two different camps, old media, new media, helping position a person well in their particular niche.

Seth: What are the three best books you've ever read that had the most impact on your work? And you're not allowed to quote the Bible or something you wrote yourself.

Joel: Okay. Gotcha. Hands down, *Category of One*. Excuse me, it's called *Becoming a Category of One* by Joe Calloway. That is a phenomenal book. I probably read it six or seven times, dog-eared, highlighted, used, abused. I love that book, *Becoming a Category of One*. *Compound Effect*, Darren Hardy. That's a phenomenal book as well, *Compound Effect*. Darren and Joe have both been on my show and are incredible mentors. I would recommend that your audience get a hold of those books and get a hold of their audio and their teachings because those people are phenomenal. For the third book, I would have to say – I want to think about this for a minute. I would say the third book is *Seven Habits of Highly Effective People* and that's Stephen Covey. It's nothing new for your audience I'm sure, Seth. A lot of people probably refer to that book as one of the greats that's out there and continues to just be a game changer.

Seth: Absolutely. I would agree with that. I greatly appreciate your time. I know how busy and successful you are. So to take some time out to share with our listeners, we really appreciate that. Of course, we will send them all to go get the ReLaunch podcast and follow everything that you do. Joel, it's been an honor and a privilege to get to spend some time with you and pick your brain. Thank you so much for doing the interview.

Joel: Appreciate your time, Seth. Thanks for your time.

INTERVIEW WITH
SCOTT PATON

Seth: Welcome to the Direct Response Marketing Magic podcast. I am your host, Seth Greene. And today, I have the great fortune of interviewing podcaster extraordinaire, Scott Paton. Scott, welcome to the show.

Scott: Hi Seth. Happy to be here.

Seth: We greatly appreciate it. I'm going to make you go back in time a little bit and ask you, how did you get started?

Scott: I got started kicking and screaming, resisting it with every fiber of my being. It was the spring of 2005 and unfortunately the owner of the company I worked for passed away. He was only 35 years old and the people that took over were afraid that the company would go down because he was so closely associated with the company. So they decided to go around the world and do boot camps on internet marketing and they asked me to speak for two hours on blogging on a Saturday night. And I knew one thing and that was if after sitting for 12 hours listening to my boss and then having this big meal and then listening to me for two hours didn't put them to sleep, nothing would. I need to talk about something else and I've been hearing about podcasting. And I thought, ah, I don't want to learn this. I'm overwhelmed with learning. And then to may shock and amazement, in 20 minutes after I decided well, I should just do it and see, I had one up and had downloaded it and had been working. And I was just amazed at how easy it was.

Seth: And what happened? So you had one up. You got started. What did you originally start out podcasting about? Were you the one doing the show? Or were you interviewing other people?

Scott: To promote the internet. Actually, I interviewed my new boss and it was an internet marketing podcast because the company was an internet marketing center. So I just talked about things that were going on in the world of internet marketing.

Seth: And were you the sole person on that show? Or were you interviewing other folks?

Scott: I like interviewing other folks simply because I find the energy is easier to maintain. And I'm not a real monologue type of person. So most of the time, I'd have a co-host or I do an interview style podcast.

Seth: And do you know how many – obviously, when you started, you probably had zero listeners and you were talking to the recorder in the air. Do you know how many subscribers you have now?

Scott: Not at all. My internet marketing podcast I should say has about 75,000 subscribers and about 10,000 or 15,000 downloads per month.

Seth: That's incredible. So obviously, you're doing something right.

Scott: Yeah. Well, all I'm doing is talking for both 20 minutes and somehow people like to listen to it.

Seth: What do you wish you knew when you started that you know now?

Scott: Wow. That's an interesting question. I think really I would have to say I wish I had used Facebook and Twitter and YouTube and some of the social media sites a lot more because – I just did the podcast. I also have a weight loss podcast. And then our first year, we had 300,000+ subscribers and 3 quarters of a million downloads. And at that time, I just said I just want to see what would happen if all we did was podcast. So we did nothing. And when I think about the internet marketing one as well, we didn't do much. So I just think being able to leverage all of these social media sites when they were just starting would have just taken us to another level.

Seth: I would agree absolutely 100 percent. Other than that, I find that obviously we talk to some of the most successful marketers and podcasters and stuff like that in the world we can learn incredible lessons from their success and what they did to become successful but we can even learn more from avoiding some of the so called million dollar mistakes they have made. What has been your biggest mistake? And what have you learned from it?

Scott: The biggest mistake I think was not focusing. I did an alternative health podcast, a personal development podcast, an internet marketing podcast, a weight loss podcast, a yoga podcast. I mean it just goes on and on and on. I probably have been involved in 30 or 40 different podcasts over the last 10 years. And all I was thinking was wow, this is really interesting technology. And I found people that are really interesting and I want to do a podcast with them. And I never really focused on presenting myself as the single expert in either one of those fields or in podcasting. And now, I'm just focusing a lot more just on being the expert in podcasting. But when I look back over the 10 years or if you do a search on my name in iTunes, you'll see all of these topics. And of course, none of them fit in terms of building a singular brand. So I'm just basically all over the place. So I think focus would be absolutely the billion dollar mistake.

Seth: I will agree with that. I mean I tell our clients and I've written about it in my books that 50 percent of the success or failure of any marketing campaign which a podcast could be considered is the proper selection of, target market. So focus would be exactly that.

Scott: Yup.

Seth: Now, you've been a part of so many not only podcasts but businesses and ventures. I have to ask you as a serial entrepreneur myself, what is your biggest challenge now?

Scott: It's the same thing actually but I'm focused on focusing. I can put it that way. I'm really narrowing and narrowing and narrowing down what I'm doing.

Seth: Focused on focus. That actually could probably a good bumper sticker, focused on focusing.

Scott: There are just too many shiny objects and I'm really just saying no to – learning to say no is the biggest thing.

Seth: Learning to say no. I think that is a huge lesson considering we all probably suffer so much from shiny object syndrome.

Scott: Yeah.

Seth: Is this podcast your most successful one? Or has something else that you've done eclipsed even this?

Scott: I would say the Weight Loss and the Mind podcast was the most successful one.

Seth: The weight loss one. And second one is?

Scott: It's called Weight Loss and the Mind.

Seth: Weight Loss and the Mind. Okay. You're involved in a number of different niches obviously and I know from listening to some of your podcasts that you are a voracious learner, so how do you stay on top of all of the constant sea of change going on in every industry you're involved in?

Scott: I don't. I depend on the experts to do that. So I take the role of either the student or the reporter. I mean I do have an interest in the areas. They're not stuff that I'm not interested in which helps but what I tend to do is try to draw that information out of either the guest or the co-host and then that's how I learn.

Seth: Absolutely. What periodicals, trade journals, magazines, what do you read every month?

Scott: Yeah, I read a lot but I have an app called Zyte.

Seth: Is that the app that lets you create like almost your own curated news magazine?

Scott: It is.

Seth: I love that.

Scott: Yeah. Me too. I can just put in weight loss or internet marketing or podcasting or whatever the topics are that I'm interested in. It'll show me a bunch of articles and then if I give it a thumbs-up, it learns and it shows me more and more of those articles. I only get on it usually in the evening for an hour but then what I do is I tweet or I post on Facebook any of the articles that I think I want to delve into in more detail later and want to share with my following. So I find that in a very short period of time I have access to quite a bit of information that's usually within a day of being published on my topic.

Seth: I would agree with that. Trying to stay on top of everything with Zite is very, very helpful. What are three of the best books you've ever read that have had the most impact on your work? And you can't quote the Bible or something that you are the author of.

Scott: Well, the one that popped into my head the second you said it was *Think and Grow Rich* by Napoleon Hill.

Seth: Every single week, I do another episode and I ask that question. And without a doubt every single week, no matter who I interview that is one of the three because it has impacted so many of us in so many ways. Can you come up with two more?

Scott: Two more. Well, let me just go look at my library.

Seth: Turn around. Roll the chair over.

Scott: Anything by Seth Godin gets like 15 thumbs-up. Anything by him I just think is absolutely amazing plus they're short reads which means you can review them again, again and again. And then *Blue Ocean, Red Ocean.* I'm not sure who that was by but it's totally changed how I look at my business and how I also look at my clients' businesses.

Seth: Absolutely. Great books, great recommendations for our listeners who haven't read those yet.

Scott: Absolutely.

Seth: And you are associated with a whole lot of different things obviously, the different ventures and niches that you play in. What are you finding across the board? I know the podcast industry obviously (A) now exists, (B) has exploded. And how are you other than the fact that some of your podcasts have hundreds of thousands of followers, how are – but there might be 300 weight loss podcasts or maybe 1000 marketing podcasts. How are you differentiating yourself from all the other folks clamoring for attention?

Scott: I would say that when you look at doing a search on say weight loss in Google you'll have 100 million or a billion results pop up. I mean it's just a massive amount of information online. When you do the same sort of thing in iTunes, they'll be a fair number but not nearly as many. Because podcasts are multitasking things you're usually do something while you're listening to them, so the consumption rate gets really high. So those people who are interested in your topic, they could run through 5 or 10 or 15 podcasts every couple of months or every week. It depends on how fanatical they are about it.

And what will happen is people that like your voice and your manner and the way that you communicate will gravitate towards you. The ones that don't will go away. And I remember listening to a podcast with this lady and she had a squealy, squeaky, scratchy voice that just grated on me and I thought she was terrible. It came up in a conversation and the person that I was talking to said, "I love her, all that she shares and the way she shares it." I just shut up and I said, "Wow, like everybody has things that they like and things they don't like." Just because I don't like it doesn't mean they're not a lot of people that do like it.

So I really think that if you just spend – this is what I tell everybody. Spend 20 minutes a day talking about something with somebody or by yourself about something that you like that involves your business. I mean you could totally do it as a volunteer hobby but I don't think you need to. You'll help people that listen to it and then it grows. They'll share it and you tell your friends on Facebook and Twitter. And all of a sudden, it will just grow and you need to – a friend of mine said this about YouTube. He said, you do a video and you do a video and you do a video and you got one view and one view and two views. And then all of a sudden after months, you've got like 10,000 views. I think it's kind of the same with podcasting. You just keep putting that information out and then people share it. And the people that like you and are your community and are your tribe or however you want to describe your following, it will grow because they will share it with their friends and their friends and their friends.

And I think – and I've seen that where we've had a huge jump in listeners and it's like, why? And then we figure out, oh, it was this person on this blog. And I went three times to the post where she said nice things about our podcast. And it was only on the third time I actually found the link I was looking for but it wasn't underlined. And I was like, how did any of these people find the link? I don't know but they did. Clicked through and they subscribed. So that's what I think is the most important part of this.

Seth: That is great feedback and a great advice. For our listeners who are resonating with what you're saying and your amazing and incredible journey, is there a website you want them to go to so they can get more from you or a particular podcast you want them to subscribe to?

Scott: I have a fairly new website I just launched called powerpodcasters.com. And from there, I put a number of hangouts that I've done that – it's basically focused on how to improve your podcasting but there's also a link to my brand new Power Podcast course as well as a good discount over the regular price for anyone that wants to check it out.

Seth: Okay. Well, thank you so much. It's been an honor to interview you. We've been here with Scott Paton, podcast extraordinaire of powerpodcasters.com and many other places I'm sure you can find online. Thank you so much. It's been an honor and a privilege.

Scott: Thanks Seth. I appreciate you having me.

INTERVIEW WITH
NIK PARKS

Seth: Today, it is my good fortune to be interviewing Nik Parks who is the Co-founder of Launching Creative. Nik thanks so much for being on the show.

Nik: Yeah. Thank you so much for having me, Seth.

Seth: We are honored to have you. You've interviewed some of the most amazing people, everyone from Bob Burg, John Dumas, and Amy Porterfield. You've appeared in Forbes, you've been all over the internet, the media and the podcasting world. So let me ask you how you got started.

Nik: It's such a really good question. So pretty much how it started was my business partner and I, David Rock, kind of just hanging out and literally playing board games. We kind of just connected and we both saw this problem that was so common among creatives and among artists as far as struggling financially, being a starving artist. And we were just wondering like, what's the cause of this problem? Why do we just expect to struggle? And it kind of grew from there. We started looking for resources and for answers and then we finally realized there's really nothing out there. So maybe we should blog about it and the blog kind of evolved into the podcast. And then through that, we were able to just make some really wonderful connections and connect with some of the people you mentioned on the podcast. It's just been a really crazy journey.

Seth: How have you grown your base?

Nik: Honestly, it's just been through social media and it's just been through building relationships. I mean, I think kind of the big thing that we really implemented is what Gary Vaynerchuk is talking about, Twitter is a cocktail party. We're kind of taking that with other platforms as well. Instead of just kind of link bombing everyone to check out our blog, check our new post, five reasons to do this, we've kind of just tried to connect with people and ask questions, answer questions. And then once that relationship is kind of built, they check it out on their own. They kind of check out our website and they seem to like it.

Seth: I can see why.

Nik: Thanks.

Seth: You're very welcome. For your own podcast, how do you select and find guests. For podcasters, that seems to be one of their biggest concerns. It's who do I get in my show and how do I get them on my show. And I know you're really good at doing that.

Nik: Thanks Seth. I'm sure you know that is very time consuming and it can be very difficult as well. For me, I guess I kind of just already had this list of entrepreneurs and writers and podcasters that I already admired. And when I first started, I was like, "No, there's no way they'll be on my show." But I ended up just kind of reaching out here and there and was just repeatedly just shocked, I mean, pleasantly surprised but shocked at their generosity.

So many people would say "yeah, sure, I'd love to be on your show." And they're doing this when they weren't gaining anything from it especially before as we were building our audience. I mean, they were just being very generous with their time. And it was kind of a snowball effect. We learned that once we had a few people on our show had some clout, other people kind of saw that and they're like "oh, you know, if this entrepreneur was on it and it was worth their time, then it would be worth my time. So yeah, I'll be on your show as well." But they never phrased it like that. We just saw kind of a snowball effect and it actually became easier and easier to get people on the show. We weren't really facing a lot of rejection.

Seth: Yeah. It's always nice.

Nik: I think it also helps because we were also finding people who had something that they were putting out there. Maybe it's a new book and we kind would help you put the word out. Or maybe they have their own business. They have some kind of product or service. So for them, I mean, they kind of see this as "oh, this is a way to kind of get the word out. This is like some PR for me."

Seth: That's something also that we found. But some of our listeners would be surprised that some of the most successful people on the world, (those impossible to reach, top of the mountain folks that you think of) are the most generous and the most willing to help and responded when you had five listeners and said, "Of course, I'll be on your show. If one person gets something out of it, then I did my job. And you get someone like Jack Canfield on the show. And then of course, that turns into well now, you have 5000 subscribers that month because Jack was on your show. And it's just an incredible, incredible journey up the ladder for lack of a better term.

Nik: Yeah, absolutely. I think the people are so successful because they're so generous. And it's just one of those counterintuitive things because you think that they wouldn't be here, they couldn't be here, they wouldn't have time. Yeah, I still get just amazed. I'm like, "Wow, they're just so generous and so awesome." And it's very inspiring to me.

Seth: I also want to give back as well as we get more and more successful. What do you wish you knew when you started that you know now?

Nik: I guess I would say, to just kind of slow down. I mean, I think for me and I think a lot of creatives are this way, we're definitely just ideas people, so always thinking of the new idea. "Oh, I want to do this as well. Let's feature this. Let's try this new thing. Let's start this new project." But I would end up stretching myself too thin. I was starting a lot of projects and then I couldn't finish them, I couldn't see them through. And I've learned that it's actually better to just kind of do it slow and steady. You have a few things that you've started and you are just following through and you're actually executing instead of just taking all these shiny objects and then just dropping them. Yeah, I would say I would've wanted to be a little more patient and say, "You know what, its okay. We're just doing one, two, three things, you know, instead of 20 different things and being on 20 different platforms."

Seth: How are you combating what we call shiny object syndrome?

Nik: Yeah, I guess I'm just trying to be more disciplined. And I think it's just small steps. And I'm being intentional and just listening to other interviews and watching other videos on YouTube where I see people who are much further along in their careers, they're much more successful than where I am. And they're kind saying the same thing, you know, just slowing it down realizing that I do need to take time to rest. I do need to just kind of enjoy life. And I'm thinking, "Okay. Well, if they're saying that's true and if that's worked out for them, then it should be true for me as well." And so I think it's just kind of small victories every day instead of thinking, "Okay, I'm just going to totally change the way I think and have this fundamental change overnight." You know what else helps though is having a list. And as much as I love techie things and anything web, I still do it on just a piece of paper. And it might be something as small as just five things to do that day and I literally cross them off when I accomplish them. And that helps me stay focused as well.

Seth: Absolutely. And it certainly provides a type of gratification when you get to actually cross something off.

Nik: It does feel good. And actually oftentimes, I will – if I start my list late in the day, I'll actually write things down that I've already accomplished that day and immediately cross them off. It just kind of makes me feel more accomplished.

Seth: I understand. What has been your biggest mistake? And what did you learn from it?

Nik: That is a really good question. I guess I would say the biggest mistake – I mean maybe that's a good thing I can't really think of like a huge devastating thing which is probably good. But then again, I'm not really thinking of a take away, of a good learning experience. Yeah, I guess maybe for me I would say the biggest mistake I probably made and that might go along with what I was saying was just taking time and just enjoy life more. I actually can map this out my head and put a timeline.

October was when I finally took a vacation with my wife and we just had a getaway. We got out of the city because we live in New York City. And like, we completely unplugged from social media. We had our phones on airplane mode the whole time. And I think its very eye opening to me because then I realized, "Oh my gosh, like, there's so much more to life. And I'm not using my computer and my phone and I'm not stressed out and I'm not trying to balance like a million other things." And so I would say, yeah, probably my biggest mistake was just thinking that, I have to be successful as soon as possible. Instead I was realizing success is the journey and it's not the destination and yeah, just taking life a little more easy.

Seth: I know you've got probably more irons in the fire that I can count. What is your biggest challenge now?

Nik: I guess my biggest challenge now is – yeah, I guess being focused, like kind of prioritizing and realizing, okay, what takes priority right now? When you have a lot of irons in the fire, you kind of think, which one do I need to focus on? Because it really can get distracting. And with any business, there are aspects that you don't really enjoy, the parts that just aren't really that much fun to you. And then you have the other aspects that are just a blast. Like, if I can do this all the time, that would be amazing.

And, I don't know, part of me thinks, well, maybe you do kind of reach that level where you're able to kind of delegate those parts that you don't like. But when you have too many irons in the fire, it can become very distracting and you can get so carried away in it that you're not really seeing any progress in anything because you're not doing the nitty gritty things that need to get done.

Seth: Absolutely. I know from following you that you're a voracious learner. With everything that's going on in the industry and everything that keeps changing which is constantly, how are you staying on the cutting edge?

Nik: For me, it's kind of just being willing to just make mistakes because it does; it changes so quickly like you're saying. Something that I've quoted before, it was a quote I heard from Barbara Corcoran, she's on Shark Tank. And she was being interviewed on Entrepreneur on Fire which is John Lee Dumas' podcast and she was saying, "You don't have to get it right. You just have to get it going." And so I've really tried to live by that because it just spoke to me so much. It really resonated with me.

So much is changing all the time. You just kind of go out and do it. And if you do make mistakes, if you do it incorrectly, it's not going to be the end of the world and you're still learning something new and you're learning how not to do this. It's kind of like the old Thomas Edison story that we all knew about inventing the light bulb that he made mistakes. I think it's just kind of like there's this new platform that came out or there are new changes in the social media channel and whatever. The ones who are just really, really savvy and the ones who really are on the forefront, they're just kind of doing it. They're not really sitting there and thinking about it and theorizing. It's kind of like just run out in the battle and just make some mistakes.

Seth: It was funny that you mentioned Barbara. I've done some consulting for some of the sharks. And I had the good fortune of being with her at an event. And one of my biggest writer downer was something she said, somebody asked her a question about "how do you balance it all?" And she said "balance is bullshit. Boundaries rule." And she said one of her examples of boundaries is she has a cell phone that is only for work. The second she walks in the door at home, she physically turns it off, not vibrate but powers it down and won't turn it on again until she leaves the house the next morning.

And I said, "Wow, I want to be like you when I grow up." I haven't figured that out on how to pull that off but I've gotten better. I have now taken my email off my phone which of course did not do wonders for my mental state trying to get some sleep. And I found just deleting my email accounts from my phone made a significant difference but I haven't figured out how to completely cut the cord and turn it off yet.

Nik: That's funny. And it really makes you think because especially someone like Barbara Corcoran who would just have so much more to lose. I mean, talk about someone who's accomplished so much and has such extremely high net worth and has so many things going on. And that's kind of encouraging to me. I'd think okay, if she's able to completely turn off that phone and her empire didn't crumble overnight –

Seth: Right. It's might be like a $2 million deal or $20 million deal or a CNBC appearance or one of the businesses that she owns is having a crisis and she says you know what, it can wait. Nobody is going to die if I don't pick up the message until tomorrow.

Nik: Yeah. That really puts it in perspective. It's like – all right, I don't know if I have anything like that going on. So maybe, I should be able to do that. Things will still be okay in the morning.

Seth: What are three of the best books you've ever read that have had the most impact on your work? And you're not allowed to quote the Bible or a book you wrote yourself.

Nik: I love those rules. I would say *How to Win Friends and Influence People* by Dale Carnegie. That is a book that literally changed my life. I think I was very, very, very, very, very awkward. I just really struggled socially before that and it really helped me to just understand people. Like, "oh, this is what I need to do to connect with people and this is what I'm doing wrong." I read that one in college. I actually go back and reread it. I try to reread it every year that was an unbelievable book. Let's say another one was *Rework* and Jason Fried.

Seth: Yeah, he is awesome. I'm looking at it on my shelf right now.

Nik: That was a good one too. I also just love how it's just a fun book and he had these quirky pictures and just kind of charts but that was a really, really good one. It's all about just kind of stripping everything down and just kind of being lean and just streamlining things. It was a really cool book. And these guys at 37 Signals a massively successful company. Their employees work remotely and they work four days a week. That's crazy, crazy cool but that was just crazy to me.

And I would say the third one would be probably the *E-Myth Revisited* by Michael Gerber. That was a good one too because that totally changed my mindset as far as – okay, here's the difference between a freelancer and an entrepreneur. I need to figure out how to put systems into place because I'm not doing everything on my own and I'm not wearing all these hats.

Seth: Absolutely. I know there are in your niche, not just on the podcasting side but obviously in everything you're doing for clients, there are plenty of firms who claim to do some of what you do. What would you say is your most compelling differentiation factor?

Nik: There's something to be said about really just kind of being in the trenches and being small and being lean. I think when you really are small, you can really shift gears very, very quickly. I mean, if something goes horribly wrong, you can just make a decision and change. And I've definitely had experienced where I worked for large organizations and it was just ridiculous how long it would be for anything to get finished. I mean, there's just so much red tape that I have to go through different departments and I have to get approval. I couldn't believe it. I couldn't believe that's the way these organizations are run.

When you're just kind of this lean company, you can just say, "You know what, that didn't work. Let's do this." And that's as complicated as it gets. I feel like when clients have skin in the game, like when their money is at stake, that's probably, I would think, pretty encouraging to them to just know okay, look guys, they fixed it super quickly and they're going to do a good job now instead of thinking well I'm still throwing money at this.

Seth: I think that makes a lot of sense. Well, I greatly appreciate your time. I've got two pages of notes. I'm sure our listeners do too. This has been a fascinating interview with Nik Parks, Co-Founder of Launching Creative. For our folks who are resonating with what you're sharing and they want more from you, where do you want us to send them? Do you want us to send them to the Launching Creative podcast, to the Launching Creative website? What's the best place for them to go to get more from you?

Nik: Yeah. Just launchingcreative.com. And they'll definitely be able to find us there. And yeah, we have a lot of content. So they're definitely welcome to check it out. Yeah, I think they'll like what they find and I appreciate the plug.

Seth: Thank you so much.

INTERVIEW WITH
SCOTT MANN

Seth: Welcome to the Direct Response Marketing Magic podcast. I am your host as always, Seth Greene. Today, I have the good fortune of interviewing Scott Mann. Scott, welcome to the show.

Scott: Hello, Seth. Thanks for having me on to talk about my work as a podcaster.

Seth: Absolutely. Well, let me ask you, how did you get started?

Scott: I got started because I was learning about ecological design. I have a background in Computer Science and realized that there was this missing niche. There were some folks who were doing work about agriculture and sustainable age around 2010 but there wasn't a lot of work really about how people get involved in doing small scale work in their own backyard. So I combined my love of ecology and agriculture and computer science and kind of blended them together to get things going.

Seth: And how did you get into podcasting?

Scott: It was from going to some classes. I was talking to some of my fellow students had background in Technology. So as we're having those conversations, I saw a need to start talking about this stuff in order to reach a larger market. So I went ahead and I just took some old computer equipment I had, some friends who I knew who did web hosting and things, grabbed a cheap mic and started recording.

Seth: And obviously, you've grown significantly since then.

Scott: Yes, quite a bit. Back in the beginning, it was interesting as I thought that I was the only person listening to my own show mostly because I had to edit the episodes. And then after a couple of months, I started seeing my numbers take off. And then after the first year, I had about 300 regular listeners to me every time that I release an episode. Now, after taking some time off, I came back to it after a year. I was surprised I had more listeners after I had taken a vacation than when I did when I've been doing it full time. And that showed that there was really a need for it. And my show has grown 10-fold since that return. And I was really impressed last year in making a switch from being kind of like just an amateur podcaster doing it as a hobby to making it kind of my part-time vocation. I wound up with reaching 125,000 people last year and having 800,000 downloads.

Seth: That's a really incredible growth rate.

Scott: Yes, very much so. And for such a small niche, I was really surprised to see that kind of growth.

Seth: I can understand that. Let me ask you this. How did you grow? I mean obviously the word spread. But did you do any specific strategies on marketing of the podcast to help it achieve that growth? Or was it all just organic?

Scott: It started out really organically but then I saw that my best engagement was through social media. The more that I tweeted, the more that I posted at Facebook and interacted with my audience, the more that it allowed me to kind of build a relationship with those people who were tuning in every week and the more that I became a fixture in that community and being an active part of it rather than just kind of a passive producer but involved in active engagement. That really provided an opportunity for me and the audience to get to know one another better. I started putting out my direct phone number and an email address and asking people to contact me if they ever had questions. They started doing that.

Along with that, I also started doing some advertising using Facebook and Google just to put a couple of small ads up there when I was getting some traction on some particular posts either on Facebook or my website to promote those. This is what they wanted to learn more about. This is what they wanted to hear. So by promoting that, that got more people engaged with these very active vibrant pieces that my audience was saying they wanted more of.

Seth: Always a good idea to give them what they want.

Scott: Very much so. And actively asking my listeners for feedback also helped in the early days when I was just kind of sitting in my office recording and producing and putting things out there because that let me find out how to better establish my niche. And through that, that's how my interview style developed because I don't do a 20-question style interview. It's more conversational because that's what I found people like. That's when my own voice came through and I was able to connect with people even better.

Seth: Do you select and how do you find your guests? I know for a lot of podcasters starting out that's one of their concerns.

Scott: Well, I'll take you at the very beginning. In the first days when I was looking for guests, I happened to get a book from a publisher that I just really enjoyed that was within the niche that I fill. So I just interviewed that author, Rachel Kaplan. And then, from that, I just asked her, who are some people you know who are doing this kind of work that you would recommend I talk to? And then it was just every recommendation I got from somebody I will send them an email and just like, hey, I talked to this person. They said that I should contact you. Would you like to do an interview? Yes or no? And if somebody said yes, great, I would schedule an interview. That allowed me to get to know more the people in my particular community that I didn't know about previously.

And now, it's kind of reached the point where years later I'm getting contacted by people who want to be interviewed and I'm getting contacted by various publishing houses if they're looking to promote authors. "Here's a copy of the book. Read it. Let me know if you want to talk to them." I'm having now publishing houses set up interviews for me with their people. But I still continue to go back to my audience and members of the community and go, "who do you want me to talk to?" And then I go through those lists and go, okay, well, I'll talk to this person or maybe that person isn't a good fit. And now, I can be a bit more selective about who I have on the air based on my one interview a week production schedule.

Seth: What is your biggest challenge?

Scott: Time. I think one of the biggest things that a lot of folks who are doing, who are interested in podcasting and doing this kind of work is that in order to produce a high quality show doing one episode an hour a week style that I do is about 20 hours' worth of work. By the time I contact a guest, line up the interview, figure out what questions I'm going to ask and everything else. In addition to the podcast, I'm also a full-time Dad. I'm the primary stay-at-home parent as well as a graduate student. So fitting all that in and trying to do podcasting in ecological design and education as my career, that's where it comes down and just trying to manage all of that and to schedule my priorities and schedule my time.

And sometimes because of the different hats that I wear, certain things need to be adjusted. Sometimes, an episode doesn't make it out on time. Or sometimes, I have to skip an episode. But again, whenever I have to do that, if I let the audience know, that flexibility is not an issue. And often, it's because I'm honest about having these other responsibilities in my life that builds this greater engagement because I'm a human being behind the microphone, not just someone who's producing something like a machine. And it continues to help me engage and grow my audience.

Seth: That's good advice. I know with all you've got going on you are a voracious learner. What do you do every month to stay on top of all of the trends that keep changing? It seems like almost every day in your industry and in podcasting.

Scott: I find that Twitter is a huge help. By engaging with other people who are professionals in this field, I can spend a couple of minutes every day just going through my Twitter feed by following the right people and seeing what articles they're posting, what work they're doing. And that's allowed me to build a network of people worldwide who are doing this work so that we can assist one another. I also subscribe to a couple of industry magazines. That really helps. They're a bit more topical and aren't necessarily as general as what I might do on any given week but that really helps as well as just staying engaged with the people who are publishing the books in this industry. Chelsea Green, Timber Press are some of those, are the ones who are very active within my field. And just knowing what they're going to be coming out with really helps because I've gotten to watch the way that trends have moved since I began in 2010 when it was a lot of backyard and home scale kind of stuff and then we moved to mushrooms for a while. And now, the conversation is moving more towards like social work and community building. And if I hadn't been following what those different groups were working on and what materials they were pushing, I think that I would still be talking about backyard garden design and not be looking at these larger trends.

Seth: What are three of the best books you've ever read that had the most impact on your work? And you can't quote the Bible or something you are the author of.

Scott: I love Masanobu Fukuoka's *The One-Straw Revolution* because even though he's talking about farming, his idea is that. It's about cultivating human beings. And I think that every career path or anything that we do is that kind of an endeavor, that when you really, really engage, it begins to change you, that it's just not about the work that you do. But it's about the impact that it has on your life.

A particular author whose work that I continue to follow is Derrick Jensen, the author and activist, because a lot of his work and the way that it relates to the work that I do with the environment has just opened my eyes to more than just what happens on the news. And I had the opportunity to interview him and a lot of his work is about getting us to question what it is that we're doing, the actions that we take. And again, even though he's an environmental author, I feel that it has a broad application, his work to anybody's field because he gets us to ask better questions about the choices we're making. And even something as simple as, "is what I'm doing in this moment actually helping my career or any particular goal that I'm working on?"

And the last one is just a classic, Barbara Winter's *Making a Living Without a Job* because when you step out onto that limb of wanting to be an entrepreneur especially someone who doesn't have an entrepreneurial spirit. So I never felt that I could be running a successful podcast or really any kind of successful venture and realizing that what we're doing feeds us, feeds our family, feeds our soul while still reaching the right people in order to do the work that we care about.

Seth: I think that this is absolutely fascinating. I greatly appreciate your time and the interview. For our listeners who want to get more from you, who are resonating with what you're saying, where would you like us to send them? Do you want us to go to the podcast, to your website? Where do you want them?

Scott: I would love them to go to the podcast website. They can find out more about the kinds of topics that I cover and the things that I engage in. But I also encourage anyone after listening to this or checking out that information to give me a call. My website is the *permaculturepodcast.com*. My phone number if anybody wants to reach out to me is 717-827-6266. I make that publicly available to answer questions for anybody at any time though I don't always answer. So leave a voicemail and I'll get back to you.

Seth: You're the only guest I've ever had who gave out his phone number. That is absolutely incredible and a testament to how much you want to help people. This has been a fascinating interview. Scott, I greatly appreciate your time.

Scott: Thank you and have a great day.

INTERVIEW WITH
JEFF BROWN

Seth: Can you tell us a little bit about what you're doing? How you're helping folks? I know you're making a difference. Go for it.

Jeff: My Podcast is called the Read to Lead Podcast. I interview successful and inspiring business book authors with a new episode weekly typically, every Tuesday. About a year or maybe 14 months ago, I began helping people enter the podcasting space leveraging my background and career, two and a half decades in radio and what I've learned there and helping folks apply some of those techniques to podcasting as a podcast coach and mentor. So those two things have gotten the primary focus of my attempt to the last year plus.

I'm an avid reader and it's something that I've been passionate about for 12 or 13 years and was kind of frustrated that more people weren't taking advantage of the knowledge and wisdom that was out there. The stats in this country on reading when you look at them, they are very abysmal. Very few people read with any sort of regularity or intentionality and that was something I wanted to try and change. Plus I loved talking about what I was learning with other people and sharing that process along the way. And then, to the chance to sit down with some of our countries brightest minds would be really cool. And so, a podcast for me was a way to kind of scratch all of those itches at the same time. And so, around the spring of 2013, I begin to plan to launch and in July 2013, it finally went live.

Seth: Congratulations I know you had a lot of success but how have you grown your subscriber base over the last couple of years so rapidly?

Jeff: It's really about consistency and hard work. Often times, I can be guilty of setting goals and then when I don't hit those come into the conclusion that well, I've failed because I didn't hit that goal. And sometimes, maybe I didn't set a very good goal or I didn't set a very reasonable goal. And so, it just can be a matter of re-evaluating where I'm at and understanding that well, I haven't failed at this. I just need a pivot or I need to reset and so I've been able to do that along the way. And as small milestones have happened for my podcast, I feel like I've been pretty good about leveraging those milestones and typically what happens with most podcasting journeys is this - it starts to grow and then you hit a plateau and it kind of levels out for a while. And then if you have a couple of successes here, there may be a growth to the next plateau. It's sort of a stair step kind of process. A lot people get frustrated with that.

I talked to a podcaster, a client of mine just a few weeks ago, and in our first session and they were lamenting the fact that their podcast hasn't taken off like they had expected it to and they were down the dumps. And I say, "Well, when did you launch?" And they said six months ago and I said you need to give it a little more time because this isn't an overnight kind of a thing.

Seth: You mean, they didn't hit iTunes New and Noteworthy overnight?

Jeff: Not exactly. It is certainly possible but you have to really be intentional about it. And some folks were seeing others successes that people are having and thinking, "Oh, I can jump into this and I can emulate that same success". And oftentimes, your results aren't typical and so you have to be very methodical, you have to be very intentional about what you're doing and you also have to very passionate about your topic. If you're not, and if you're doing this to build an audience exclusively or try to get noticed, then those are oftentimes the wrong reasons. You really need to be doing it for the love of it. The love of the medium and the love of the topic or world that you are espousing, and that's really what's going to draw people to you. And then, as you have little milestones of successes, you need to leverage those and not be afraid to, you know, say occasionally at least, "Look at me and look at this awesome thing that's happening".

Seth: A lot of people probably have the wrong expectations going in which sort of sets them up. A lot of podcasters when they're starting out are concerned about it. How are you finding great guests for your show?

Jeff: A lot of folks are overwhelmed by the process or think that you have to be some sort of special club to get the attention of some of these folks. And this is really where consistency and maybe to a large extent, persistence comes in. You don't want to be a pest certainly but oftentimes, when you reach out to someone who is very busy, who is maybe well-known let say, you may not get a 'yes' the first time around. But oftentimes, if you read between the lines, sometimes the 'no's' are really more like not like right now, than they are actually 'no's'. And so, if you can recognize that for what it is, and not be afraid to a few months down the road re-engage that person, over time you're likely to be successful.

I've had the opportunity, for example, to interview one of my favorite authors Seth Godin. Well, Seth said 'no' essentially the first few times I asked him but what those answers really were, were "Well, now is not a really good time, maybe in the future." I held on to that and made sure that the next opportunity may present itself, I was out there to make that request. And eventually, Seth did say 'yes'. And so, that's a big part of it. Also, just taking advantage of the opportunity to participate in the communities of the people you're reaching out to.

If your first interaction with them is you asking them for something, then don't be surprised if you get a 'no'. But if they instantly, you know, if your name has a familiarity or they recognize that you're somebody who has brought value to their community in the past, not expecting anything in return, they're going to be far more likely to say 'yes' to you.

And so, I have made it a point to always be trying as much as I can to be promoting other people's stuff ten times or more as often as I promote my own stuff. And its sort of that old axiom - what goes around, comes around. When it comes to reaching out to people, it's also important to think creatively and try some things that maybe at the beginning you're not sure whether or not they'll work. I wanted to have Gary Vaynerchuk on my show.

Seth: Gary is one the kings of social media and podcasters and everybody hopefully knows the story of Wine Library TV. Gary would be an amazing coup and of course, if he goes and to tweets out, "Hey, I'm on Jeff's show." You know, you get maybe a hundred thousand more subscribers.

Jeff: Well, you know potentially…

Seth: You can hope.

Jeff: Yeah, you can hope, yeah. And now, I got a little creative with Gary. The first couple of times I read stuff to Gary I think by email first and then by Twitter. After that, I didn't get a response and kind of all but given up on getting Gary's attention. And I participated in his community to various levels but I noticed that at the beginning of the month that I wanted to have him on, a new book that he had written was coming out called *Jab, Jab, Jab, Right Hook*.

Seth: Great book.

Jeff: At the beginning of that month, he appeared on the cover of a magazine I subscribed to. I can't remember which one it was. I took a picture of that cover and posted it on Instagram and propagated it to Facebook and elsewhere and just sort of poke fun at myself from the sense that, well, of course, Gary doesn't have time for dinner with me. He is everywhere and he doesn't need one more little guy promoting what he is doing. Who am I? He's got a lot of coverage already. Well, someone who I'd interviewed in the past, who I had connected with spins on Facebook and who also happened to know Gary and had a relationship with him saw that post. And he pointed it out to

Gary and Gary said "can you vouch for this guy in essence," and this guy said 'yes'.

And so the next thing I know, this is all happening behind the scenes unbeknownst to me but the next thing I know this mutual connection I had on Facebook says "here is the person you need to get a hold of and here's their Twitter handle". I reached out to that person and within a couple of weeks, I was on the phone with Gary just a few days before his book would release giving me enough time to turn around the interview on the day that it released which was important for me to do that because I knew that Gary would be all over mainstream media.

And so, I was able to tweet out things that day or on Facebook that day. Things like Gary Vaynerchuk's new book is out. He is appearing on Morning Joe and MSNBC, Piers Morgan Tonight on CNN and the Read to Lead Podcast. And so perception is reality and so by leveraging in that way, people look at that and went "This show must be pretty important because he is doing guest spots on all these shows." So it's all on how you frame it oftentimes.

Seth: That is incredible and I'm jealous and inspired by you. What do you wish you knew when you started that you know now?

Jeff: Oh, boy. One of the things I guess I would say in answer to that is when I started, it never occurred to me, and I don't know why. I'm a little embarrassed to admit this but it never occurred to me that I would be sought after as a guest on other podcasts. It didn't occur to me. I was going to be this guy who interviewed so and so and so, I never thought that people would want me on their show. And so, I wished I would have recognized that opportunity earlier and had taken advantage of it earlier than I did.

I appear on podcasts now fairly regularly which is great and to me it's one of the best ways to introduce new people to your show. You know, people already listening to podcasts are the easiest group of people to get to listen to your podcast because they've already overcome the hurdles of the technology. When you appear on the podcast and get in front of other podcast listeners that don't yet know who you are, bringing them to your show is real easy.

Seth: That is a great strategy. What is your biggest challenge now?

Jeff: I think one of my biggest challenges is I pride myself on reading each authors book before I chat with them. And life often likes to get in the way and interrupt my opportunities to read. And so, I'm in a place right now where I'm not able to have numerous shows in the can like I used to. I think I actually love two in the can right now which is actually unusual. Usually, I'm doing an interview on a Monday that I'm going to turn around and publish on Tuesday and it's literally that fast. And I managed to get a couple of weeks ahead here recently but that's like I said, you caught me at a good time. That's unusual. I usually work very sort of, you know, in the moment.

I started out my podcast with seven or eight interviews in the can and worked ahead. But then like I said, life gets in the way and those things catch up with you and then when you do the kind of show I do where you're putting in a pretty good amount of research prior to the interview, it's hard to then get back in front of that. I don't mind contacting an author on a Wednesday, getting the book on a Friday, reading it over the weekend, doing interview on a Monday and then, turning them and publishing that on a Tuesday, all in less than a week. And so, that's kind of how my show, typically half a week now, from week to week to week, more often than not.

Seth: I know that you are a voracious learner. What are the best books you've ever read that had the most impact on your work? And the caveat is you cannot cite the Bible or something you wrote yourself.

Jeff: The first couple of books that come to mind, of course, Seth Godin is at the top of the list. I really liked and appreciated *Linchpin: Are You Indispensable?* I think it's one of his more personal books and I really, really like the more recent one, *What To Do When It's Your Turn?* And I also like Todd Henry's book that came out a couple years ago. He hosts the podcast called *The Accidental Creative* and his book is called *Die Empty*, how to unleash your best work every day. And then more recently Jeff Goins in a book called *The Art of Work: A Proven Path In Discovering What You Were Meant To Do*. It's a great book. And then just today, at the time we were recording this conversation Jon Acuff, has released a book called *Do Over* about career and just finding work that matters and work that you loved. It is a great book as well.

Seth: Okay. I greatly appreciate those recommendations. I haven't read all of them. So I will have my assistant on Amazon later to order them. I'm sure our listeners will like it as well. For those of you, folks, who are resonating with you and want more from Jeff, once again what's the podcast they should go subscribe to. What website should they go often for what book of yours or a product should they buy?

Jeff: Well, my website is *readtoleadpodcast.com* and I would love if you could check that out and subscribing a podcast would be awesome. I think you'll find a lot of value there, a lot of great insights from the authors that's stopping for a visit. If you're interested in launching a podcast yourself, I would love for you to consider hiring me as your coach. And the best thing to do there is for us to connect and find out if we're a great fit or not. And the best way to do that is just to email me *jeff@ readtoleadpodacst.com.*

Seth: Alright, this has been Seth Greene interviewing Jeff Brown of Read to Lead. Thank you so much for joining us Jeff. It was an honor to get to spend some time with you.

Jeff: Thank you, Seth. I really appreciate it.

INTERVIEW WITH
THOM SINGER

Seth:	Today, I have the good fortune to be interviewing Thom Singer.
Thom:	Hi, Seth. Thanks for having me.
Seth:	Thanks so much for being here. Let me ask you this, let's start at the beginning. How did you get started?
Thom:	Well, I guess at the very beginning, I actually was born in the suburbs of Los Angeles and I grew up in L.A, went to San Diego state and became a professional photographer doing weddings and corporate events. I was working for a guy and he sent me to a conference for event photographers, and I met another guy who had a business in Texas. He said, "I want you to come and be manager." So when I was 25 years old, I up and moved with my girlfriend from the bay area in California to Austin, Texas thinking I would stay two years, then I would go somewhere and start my

own photography business. That didn't really work out that way.

I got to Austin and we fell in love with the city of Austin, but the company I was working for hit some hard times, I got laid off. I sort of went into this bounce around career. I went to work for the Chamber of Commerce. I went to work for an association. I did a couple of different things. I was a stay-at-home dad when my youngest daughter was born. Then I became the marketing director for a very large firm.

While I was at the law firm, one of the things the managing partner asked me to do was to create a class for the lawyers on how to network better. I thought, "Oh, they're going to hate this because there was no CLE credit for it." The lawyers, they didn't want to listen to their marketing guy to teach them how to network. I did the class and they liked it so much, they sent me on the road to the other 10 offices for that law firm.

Then I changed firms with some of the lawyers that brought me with them to a new firm. That firm sent me on the road teaching business development skills to the attorneys. I enjoyed it. They seemed to like it.

One day, one of the partners in the Washington, D.C. office, the firm that I was working for, pulled me aside after a presentation and said, "Why do you work for us?" I kind of thought was an insult, like "Why do we employ this guy? He's a buffoon." He was like, "No, you must understand because you're really good at this and you'd make more money and probably have more fun if you were out doing this." I'd love to say that day, I went out and started my own business, but it took me about another seven years. I went to work for a bank and then a consulting firm. But six years ago, I decided

I was going to become a professional speaker and trainer and consultant and I haven't looked back.

Seth: Wow. That's an incredible journey. How did you get started with your podcast?

Thom: So my podcast came about because I was at a meeting last summer for the National Speaker's Association. One of the speakers was talking about, "If you feel like you're at a plateau or you just feel you need to open your eyes to new things, go out and interview 50 people. Then write about it for your blog." He wasn't saying, "Go start a podcast", but he said that, "If you sit down and interview 50 interesting people, you will never be the same." Your curiosity of finding out about them will change your life.

So I was going to do this on my blog and I started thinking about who I wanted to interview. I really like entrepreneurs and entrepreneurship. I do a lot of work as a professional speaker and a master of ceremonies for tech companies who do users group meeting where they bring their customers in. I have a really good program that helps make that conference better. So I want to reach out to CEOs of companies that did those types of client events and I was going to write about them.

Then somebody said, "You know, that should really be a podcast instead." So I started it as Cool Things Entrepreneurs Do and I started it six months ago, and I've done about 60 interviews. The advice was right. Interviewing 50 plus people had changed me.

Seth: How have you grown your listener base since you started?

Thom: Well, I was really fortunate in the fact that I didn't just jump in and just start doing it. I actually spent a couple of months studying podcast. So I knew when I launched, I had to pay attention to my first eight weeks because iTunes will give you special credit if you can get a lot of listeners, a lot of downloads and some reviews. I don't know that I did it "the right way." I did it good enough that ended up being in the top of all career podcast during that eight-week period in a little while longer, and I ended up at the top of the new and noteworthy list on iTunes. So a lot of people check that out to see what's going. So I found a lot of listeners that way.

Then once that went away, I get a lot of it because I talk about it in my speeches. I speak about 60 times a year and I've worked in an entire module into my presentations about being curious and interviewing people. I'm not doing it under the guise of, "Hey, go start a podcast", but I'm using my podcast as an example of being able to sit down and talk to people and discover how they find their success. So I talk about it to my audiences, and oftentimes those groups then will go and download the podcast and listen to it and continue to listen to it. So I kind of have inter-mingled it into my speaking career.

Seth: That's a brilliant strategy. I know one of the things podcasters, when they're starting out, they're very, very concerned about how you select and find guests.

Thom: You know, Seth, I think that's a great question because I've listened to and talk to a lot of podcasters who are way more successful than I am. A lot of them are, "Oh, you want to be very judicious. You want people with a bigger audience than you. You want someone who is sort of the guru, who loves to go out and tweet." What I've actually found is some of the guru type people who, they're nice guys and women, but they do not spend a lot of time re-tweeting. I found a lot of them, I have them on my show and I put it out on Twitter and they'll like it. Liking it just says, "Hey Tom, I saw that", not re-tweet to my billions of followers.

Seth: Right.

Thom: So what I found is some of the regular people who don't do a lot of podcasts are the ones who were thrilled and sometimes starting to do more SEO. So I started off. I interviewed a lot of my friends, a lot of speakers, a lot of authors, a lot of consultants, a lot of people I know from the National Speaker's Association, and those people have been great because they're well-spoken, they make good guests, but I wanted to get to the point where I was interviewing more entrepreneurs and business leaders.

As I'm now getting to the point where I'm starting to do that, a lot of those people, their companies put it out on social media because their CEO hasn't been interviewed on a lot of shows, because these aren't like famous CEOs, these are guys out there fighting the good fight. I haven't been that judicious as to try and to figure out who can promote me. I've sort of done it as who would be interesting to talk to. While many of those people don't help me "grow my show", a lot of the people I interview are just regular guys working hard. They're thrilled to be on the show. Some of those people are the people who promoted me the most.

Seth: You're paying it forward and it's coming back to you.

Thom: I hope so. I mean, at the end of the day, I'm having a lot of fun talking to people. I hope I'm getting better as far as an interviewer. So, I was told years ago before I became a professional speaker that it would take 300 speeches before you could really feel totally comfortable, like "Yeah, I can do this anywhere no matter what happens." At that time,

I thought, "Three hundred speeches! God, that'll take me years!"

Now, you fast-forward nearly a decade or whatever it's been and I have done probably 450 professional level speeches and it is true. I'm really comfortable in it. So going into the podcasting, I knew it would probably take me 100 or 200 interviews before I would really feel strong. I'm only 60, so I still have a long way to go. I hope I'm getting better. The people who've listened all along tell me that I am.

Seth: Well, those are the votes that count.

Thom: That's right.

Seth: What do you wish you knew when you started that you know now?

Thom: When I started my podcast or I started my speaking career?

Seth: Let's do both. Let's start with speaking career, and then your podcast.

Thom: I wish I knew, from my speaking career, I wish I knew how long it was going to take. I sort of have this fantasy about what the speaking business is. The reason for that is, those of us who are in audiences, because I was a sales and marketing guy, so I went to a lot of conferences. The companies that I worked for planned the conferences, so I hired speakers.

What happened is, if you look at it from the outside and you think the business is one thing. I thought, "Wow, I'm going to do this and here's the way it's going to happen", because I was looking at it from a different perspective as a consumer. Once I became a speaker and had to work with meeting planners and position myself as somebody who would add value to their conference, especially because I'm not famous and I don't have a New York Times best seller and I didn't found a giant company, I had to go about it in a different way. It took me several years to be able to kind of get the momentum where I could get back to my lifestyle for my family. I wish I had really understood that the inside of the business as speaker is way different than what you see on the outside.

Seth: Very, very true. What do you wish you knew when you started your podcast?

Thom: I wish I had started my podcast six years earlier. That's all. There's all sorts of famous people and people coming out of NPR and different media things who suddenly are there. The competition to have a podcast and really find listeners, it's crazy. It's one of those things where there's just far too many people out there doing podcast to really easily get noticed.

I interviewed Jordan from the Art of Charm, and one of the things he said, he gets the question because that's one of top-rated podcasts, they say, "Wow, how do you start a podcast and have it as highly rated as the Art of Charm?" He goes, "The first step is you get a time machine and go back in time six years and podcast six years ago when there weren't that many podcasts." I laughed but I thought that's exactly right. I wish that I had started this earlier because even 18 months earlier, there wasn't the sheer amount of career in business podcasts that there are now.

Seth: Very true. It's funny that I interviewed in the previous episode a gentleman who started I believe in 2005 and was one of the first podcasters and was at the very first podcast conference with Paul Colligan instant customer and Mike King who was one of the first podcasters too, and they had a discussion 10 years ago at the very first podcaster conference, it's very small, about they were the only two people saying, "How do we monetize this now that we're starting this new platform?"

Nobody at the first conference was talking about making any money off of it. They were just talking about what microphone do we use, and what equipment are we supposed to have, and how is this going to work? Fast-forward now and that podcasting conference would have tens of thousands of people at it at the very least.

Thom: Right. Absolutely.

Seth: What is your biggest challenge? Because obviously, you've grown it. You're quite successful. You've got a million balls in the air. What's your biggest challenge now?

Thom: My biggest challenge with the podcast really is just being able to get noticed in that busy sea of business and career podcasts. My biggest challenge with my speaking career is to keep the momentum going, because you have to always have something new. I had one client talk to me about re-using me. Like, what are you doing that's new that we've never heard of? And it's like, wow, your audience wouldn't know me because it's been three years since I was there. You have turned over. But the planner didn't want anything that was similar. So it's trying to keep myself fresh and...

Seth: It's so funny that that's your answer, because I struggle with... personally, I grow, for a lack of a better term, I have been dealing with my parents who are local, let's say, a couple of times than once. My dad will say, "What's new at work?" And I'll say, "I haven't seen you in three weeks. How many ways do you want me to answer that question? I've got a list..." I normally might have answer, "Oh, nothing" or "there's lots of stuff", but I don't answer it because if I took out the list of everything we did in the last three weeks that was different from the last time I saw them, it'd probably be a couple of pages long.

Seth: I try to be nice and social but it was at my birthday. My family birthday dinner and my dad said, "What's new at work" and at first I said, "Oh, whatever. Just lots of stuff." My wife looked at me and she gave me the look like, "Be nice and engaging, please." So I said, "Well, I come up with our next three products. These are the launches that we're doing. These are the podcast people I'm interviewing. This is what marketing campaigns were sending. This is what we're doing. But here are two things that are really cool." I think halfway through, my dad's eyes, glazed over. I said, "That's why I don't answer that question."

Thom: I was going to say that it is true that if we really think about it, there are probably a lot of things that are new but it is one of the things that's hard to articulate.

Seth: Correct. Which is why I understood Bill Glazer, Dan Kennedy's former business partner told people he was an auditor for the IRS and then no one would talk to him because it took him at least half an hour to try and explain what he did. So, at first I didn't get it but it took a few years of being a serial entrepreneur that I realize that, on airplanes just saying I work at the IRS is a much better answer.

I know that you are a voracious learner and you are constantly reading and consuming content and trying to stay on top of all of the trends that are going on because it's constant change, as Gary Vaynerchuk would say. How do you stay on top of everything? How do you stay on the cutting edge?

Thom: I don't know that I do. I think that I'm always one step behind where I'd love to be, but I have two things. One is, I always try to be reading a book. I used to read 25 books a year and I found that I don't do that anymore and I think it's because I always have the phone in my hand, so I'm always looking at social media. I read a lot of articles instead of a lot of books now. But I always try to be kind of following what's going on.

The other thing is, is that I'm part of a mastermind group with five other professionals speakers or four other. There's five of us total, and one of the things is we all kind of watch out for each other, so none of us have exactly competitive business. One of us speaks in the college market. One is a weight loss expert and another one is a healthcare expert, and another person is a marketing and branding person. So he and I have similar businesses but not directly overlapped. So one of the things we do is we're always watching out for each other. So when we see something that is pertinent to one of the other four people's businesses, we will send that and we're always on the phone once a month. We meet in person twice a year. We go rent a house in some city near where we're going to be traveling. We all fly and then spend two days and kind of open up about our books, our marketing plans, talk about our personal lives, how our travel is affecting our family, whatever that is. Then you have sort of this whole board of directors and sort of therapy in each other. That helps me sort of stay abreast of ideas because I can only see my business from my eyes and I have four other people who are watching it from the outside.

Seth: You mentioned the reading question. You brought that up so I'll ask you, what are the three best books you've ever read that have the most impact on your work? You're not allowed to quote the Bible or something you are the author of.

Thom: I am a big fan of the Seven Habits of Highly Effective People. I think that that book really had a transformational affect on me. I was in my early 20s when it came out. It was one of the first business books that I really ever read or self-help style of books that I ever read. I took it to heart. I sort of got inspired by it.

Another one also old school would be Harvey McKay and probably anything that he wrote back in the '90s, Swim with the Sharks Without Being Eaten Alive. Shark-proof. Beware of the naked man who offers you a shirt. He had a whole series of best-selling books back in the '90s. I would get them on tape. My first job I have to drive around a lot and I would listen to them on cassette tape in my car.

Then I'm reading a book right now that I think is going to have that same level of effect, which is fascinating to me. It might just be that it's on my mind, but it's Brian Glazer who is Ron Howard's business partner in Hollywood. He's a producer, and he wrote a book called A Curious Mind. I've always been kind of on this whole thing of curiosity and learning. But ever since I started the podcast and asking more questions of people, curiosity has become something that is very core to my soul right now. His book is really fascinating the way he gets curious about things and how that leads him to blockbuster movies as a producer.

Seth: Awesome. I'm on Amazon right now. I'm getting that one.

Thom: You won't be sorry. It's brand new. In fact, I bought it while I was at by South by Southwest. I saw him speak and I went and bought it, so I don't even think two weeks ago at South by Southwest it was available for sale. I think it is now, but…

Seth: Thanks for your recommendation. Because you brought it up, obviously for those folks listening who are resonating with what you're saying and wants to get more from you, where should we send them? What podcast should they subscribe to? What books should they buy?

Thom: So the podcast is called Cool Things Entrepreneurs Do. If you just search from name, Thom, T-H-O-M, Singer on iTunes or search for Cools Things, I think it comes up if you just search for Cool Things, but it's Cool Things Entrepreneurs Do. I would love it if people would go and listen to the podcast because that's sort of my newest and greatest stuff. I'm interviewing all these people. Then, books, my original book was called Some Assembly Required: How to Make, Grow, and Keep Your Business Relationships. We ended up writing a spin-off book with a co-author, one for women – Some Assembly Required and Networking Guide for Women. There's one for graduates, there's one for realtors. Then, I have a little series of little tips books called The ABCs of Networking. There's one for public speaking, and there's a new one coming. There's one for entrepreneurs and there's a new one coming out for lawyers. So the ABCs of Legal Marketing will come out in May.

Seth: Awesome. Well, this has been a fabulous interview. I have pages of notes. I'm sure our listeners do too. Thank you so much. It's been an honor and a privilege to spend time with you.

8

INTERVIEW WITH
MARK ASQUITH

Seth: Welcome to the Direct Response Marketing Magic Podcast. I'm your host, Seth Greene. Today, I have the good fortune of interviewing Mark Asquith. Mark, welcome to the show.

Mark: How are you, Seth?

Seth: I am fantastic. Let me ask you this, how did you get started?

Mark: It's a long journey. So I think I've always have a bit of entrepreneurial spirit in me. I've always wanted to do something for myself. I did the usual stuff that everyone does and just didn't really enjoy it, didn't enjoy the people I was working for, and didn't have any shared visions with them. So I kind of just fell into marketing and everything else that I do just as a bit of an experimenting in doing things I enjoy. So it's been a fun journey really.

Seth: How did you get started in podcasting?

Mark: Believe it or not, the small business podcast, the *Excellence Expected*, that's not my first volume of podcasting actually. I've got another one which is called *Two Shots to the Head*, which is a geek culture podcast. Gary Elliott got me into it and I've been doing it ever since. That's probably just about a year ago actually. I started in geek culture.

Seth: How have you grown your listener base?

Mark: You know, I've tried a few things with this one. I found that that thing that really works and the one thing that I really, really continue to try and do is to build a small niche audience of people. So I've tried the usual Twitter tactics, I've tried everything that normal people tend to do when they're podcasting, promoting it left and right. But I focus really on relationship building. So speaking to people, getting to know people, share audiences with people. Not really being shy about asking and just telling people, "Listen, we've got something that we might be able to share together. How about I promote you on my audience and you promote me in your audience?" So it's kind of nice actually.

Seth: Absolutely. I know one of the questions podcasters are always asked when they're starting out, one of the things they're concerned with is how do you select and find guests for your podcast?

Mark: That's a really interesting question actually, Seth. Right in the early days, I have a bit of strategy which was trying to leverage other people's brands and trying to get some really high quality guests on. Obviously, that's a bit chicken and eggs. What I did to start was I approached some very, very high quality people I already knew to get my own base of guests already. So the first 20 that I interviewed were all people that I already had a connection or a relationship with. Then from there, I was able to use that to leverage that content and say, "Listen if anyone else is out there if you're a business person, especially in the UK or the US, that wants to have a good marketing exposure and want to position themselves, then come online." I use something called Response Source or one of the other ones. Sorry, I forgot the name. But it was just a press release outlet where you pop on their requirement for interviewees. People just book. People just are willing to come on the show.

Seth: Yes. I have found some of the people are, when you ask a lot of times, even some of the people who are the hardest to get a hold of, they might be a celebrity in their niche or even a real national celebrity, they are the most generous with their time and are willing to help.

Mark: It's really because I didn't ask them. You know, the interesting thing is that it seems to be this podcasting time of halo where you will, for example, say to someone, "Would like to go interview with our blog?" And people just won't do it. But if you say, "Listen, I've got a podcast", people seem to trip off themselves to get on it.

Seth: Yeah. Absolutely. It's been, obviously, a blessing for both us. I'll ask the dirty question, I'll get it out of the way. How are you monetizing your podcast?

Mark: That's an interesting one. Just before I answer that actually, I will say it is Response Source. The answer to the last question Response Source. So I highly recommend that one for requesting guests. So monetizing the podcast. I'm not directly monetizing that. I set out with the intent of not building, I guess, a big listenership. It didn't matter. I want to build a loyal base. But what I am doing, I'm using it to position myself. So I'm monetizing it in an indirect manner.

It positioned me in my niche of small business and it's taken into speaking gigs that I wouldn't have got. So I'm actually using it as a positioning to more than anything.

Seth: You've achieved quite a level of success. What do you wish you knew when you started that you know now?

Mark: That it's all right to be yourself Seth; that you can do what you want in your own voice, and it's all right because it doesn't matter what anyone else thinks.

Seth: That's right. "Lions do not concern themselves with the opinions of the sheep."

Mark: Right. I've never heard that. I like that.

Seth: I got that from Garrett White, the Warrior's Way, *Warrior on Fire*, is his podcast. He's amazing. I would check him out.

Mark: Absolutely.

Seth: What has been your biggest mistake and what did you learn from it?

Mark: I think early on in my career, I tried to do too much too soon. I wanted to get there too quickly. Frankly, I just didn't have the experience to do that. That was the biggest mistake that I made, just trying to false start success, but also concerning ourselves with the opinions of the sheep whilst trying to get to that success. I think those two combinations, those two mistakes combined makes a difficult year. So that's the biggest mistake, is that you can't fake up success; you have to do the hard work.

Seth: I would agree with that. I know you are a serial entrepreneur and probably have more balls in the air than I can count. What is your biggest challenge right now?

Mark: I do it on a set a time because if I got a problem with time, that's my own fault. The biggest problem is stopping having ideas and trying to focus on the one that I'm actually managing that minute. That's the biggest problem.

Seth: I know also from watching what you're doing, you are voracious learner and you are always constantly trying to stay on top of everything. The sea changes that are constantly taking place both in our industry and at large, how do you stay on top? How do you stay on the cutting edge?

Mark: I think you just got to emerge yourself with things. I've come to a conclusion a long time ago that you can't know everything and you can't even stay on top of everything. It's just so, so, so tough. But I just love the idea of surrounding myself with the right type of people so the winding permission that I need to know become prevalent if I'm right circles to be able to say, "Oh, yeah, yeah, that's something I need to know about." So that's the biggest thing, just surrounding myself with the biggest and brightest minds that I can find is the way that stayed up today is on that one. I can pick and choose the specific topics that I download that I'll be agreeing to.

Seth: Absolutely. I think that is good advice for all of us trying to keep us with way too much information right now. I know that you are a voracious consumer of information. What do you read every month? What trade journals, periodicals, magazines, newsletter, podcasts you listen to?

Mark: I have a lot of time traveling, so I try to consume all content via podcast. So basically, the usual ones in entrepreneurial is entrepreneurial face and the micro high at work. I also do a lot of listening to Pat Flynn. What I also do as well is some of the newer podcasters out there and just try and pick an episode from around just the central of their theme. So it's not the first one. It's not the most up-to-date and just get a feel for what other people are doing really. The podcasts are probably my biggest, biggest media choice in a minute.

Seth: What are the three best books you've ever read that have had the most impact on your work. The rules are you cannot quote the Bible and you cannot quote a book you wrote.

Mark: Okay then. So the top three: two biographies and one self-help book. So the self-help book is *Get Things Done* by Robert Kelsey, which is a research-based look at the psychology behind productivity and where that comes from. It doesn't assume that you are set at zero, it assume that you got it by habit and we need to reset ourselves back to zero before we can move forward. So *Get Things Done* by Rober Kelsy. Fantastic book. Fantastic guy as well.

And familiar with the two. These are actually biographies. So, the first one is the old *Steve Jobs* book by Walt Isaacson. I think that I just an absolute, absolute gem for anyone in business, any one that want to get a product out into the market. There are so many lessons to be learned from that.

Believe it or not, the third one is Arnold Schwarzenegger's biography.

Seth: Really?

Mark: Yeah. Massive, massive, massive fan of that. The reason is, he set out so many ambitions and he started with the end in mind. He knew where he wants to be from being a little boy in Austria. Everything that he has done is on route to that final goal. He's got to the very top of three distinctly different careers. He was a millionaire before he'd done any of them. So, massively inspirational book.

Seth: You know, I asked that question of every person on our podcast. That is the first book that you have mentioned that nobody else has ever mentioned. I am on Amazon right now going to get it because I've never read it. I didn't even know he had it out, and I never would have thought to buy it so this is an awesome recommendation. I greatly appreciate it. What is your most compelling differentiation factor?

Mark: We live in the world where everything's so accessible. I think not just for me and not just for you, Seth. I think just for everyone, because we can all learn services, we can all learn to provide things to our customers. I think the thing that people just need to remember is that these days, it's all right to be you. If you can be you, you will build a really, really good business because people will gravitate towards your personality. So I think that's the thing that we all do differently, just to be ourselves.

Seth: All right. Well, this has been a fascinating interview. I have a couple of pages of notes. I'm sure our listeners do too. We have been here with Mark Asquith. Mark, for our folks who are resonating with what you're saying and what your approach is, where do you want us to send them? Do you want them to go to your podcast, your website, buy your book? What is the best way for them to get more of you?

Mark: Thank you so much for asking. So yeah, the best place to go is head over to excellence-expected.com where you find links to all the podcasts, all the books and everything else that I do. So, excellence-expected.com.

Seth: Thank you so much.

Mark: Thanks, Seth.

INTERVIEW WITH
RYAN LEE

Seth: Today, I have the amazing good fortune to be interviewing Ryan Lee. Ryan is a former gym teacher turned serial entrepreneur and a co-author of *The Worst Case Scenario Business Survival Guide* and *Mastering the World of Marketing*.

Even more importantly, he is a busy father of four. I got three, so I'm not sure how he's doing it, but when he's not carpooling his kids, he's busy building businesses and writing a column at Entrepreneur Magazine. Thanks so much for being here.

Ryan: Thanks for having me, Seth. I'm ready to rock and roll today.

Seth: Okay. Awesome. Let me ask you this: how did you get started?

Ryan: How do I get started? I get started the way most people do in internet marketing. I was a recreational therapist in the Sheldon's Hospital. I think that's the usual path.

Seth: Right. I don't think I've ever heard that one before.

Ryan: Right. So that was my path. I graduated with a degree. I actually played for a living with kids for therapy, and I did sports and fitness with them. I did adapted aquatics, and I did that for about six years right out of college. On the side that whole time, I was a part-time personal trainer. I put myself through graduate school at night with the masters and exercise physiology, because I just love training.

My background, I ran track; I was a sprinter. I ran 100 and 200 meters all through high school and college, and had lot of success there. I always worked out and tried to stay fit. So I started doing part-time training and strengthening and conditioning for athletes. I wanted to build a website.

This was back in 1998. I'm not a techie by any means, so I hired my neighbor, Jonathan. He was 12 years old. I gave him 20 bucks. He used FrontPage 98 and we built a really simple website for my personal training company. It was called *Complete Conditioning*. I just wrote articles. This was back before YouTube.

Seth: Yeah, 1998. That was back before Al Gore claimed he invented the internet.

Ryan: I invented the internet. So I just start writing articles about fitness; we didn't even really have many pictures but it would have taken 20 minutes to download each picture. It just started growing. People started writing me, and then I started selling some training equipment online. I made a deal with an equipment manufacturer.

Then I was one of the first guys, might even the first to actually offer online personal training where people would send me 99 bucks and I would design a training program if they want to improve in sports performance and run faster and jump higher.

I remember I couldn't wait to take credit cards. They did a shopping cart, and then I would get the credit card number and I would have write it by hand on these little carbon-copy papers and use that little machine we have to slide it over with your hand and then bring it to the bank and deposit it. I mean, that's how I got started.

Things just kept growing and growing. I got bought up by a big internet company. They gave me $500 in cash, and I'm not kidding, but a lot of stock. Then I was hired and then two months later, I was fired. They fired everyone because the whole internet crash and blah, blah, blah.

Then I became a gym teacher, still building this on the side. I had a big breakthrough when I just kept hacking away and I'm like, "You know, I'm doing this. I'm going to make a go with this." I lacked a paid membership site in 2001.

Seth: One of the first membership sites.

Ryan: It was a paid membership site. It was definitely the first for strength and conditioning. The first month of the gate, it took like six grand in profits and I'm like, "Wow, this is good". I continue to work full-time at my job as a gym teacher and I just kept growing and growing and growing until the point after six or seven months, I told my wife, "Let's do this full-time". This is right before we had kids.

Now, here I am 14 years later, still doing it. I still have some health and fitness companies and supplement companies, but now I'm more known as the guy who teaches other people how to build these passion-based lean, fun, profitable lifestyle businesses. Now I'm on this podcast. I'm at the pinnacle right now.

Seth: Well, I'll have to send you your check it the mail for the flattery. Thank you. I appreciate that.

Ryan: Yes, please.

Seth: So I have found that a lot of our guests have learned more from their mistakes than they do from their successes. So if you could go back in time, what do you wish you knew then that you knew now?

Ryan: I would have focused more on really digging in earlier on to paid traffic. I was one of the early ones to do paid traffic. There was a search engine called Go To and then they became Overture and then they've been bought 10 times. But this is before Google did any paid advertising. I was able to buy clicks for like a penny each.

But once Google started doing it, it started getting more complex and complicated, and I just said, "Forget that. I'm just going to do what I do best", which is content creation, offline deals, speak at events. We've hired media buyers which has done well for us, but I would have probably focused even more on paid advertising.

Seth: Excellent. What has been your most surprising success?

Ryan: It's a great question. Surprising?

Seth: Where you didn't expect it and you're like couldn't believe it worked.

Ryan: That's a tough one, because if I do something, I'm like, "This thing is going work." So I never come in thinking, "Ah, it won't work". I mean, I've had products I've launched where I didn't think they would do quite as well.

I did a product years ago called Nano Continuity, which is about how to create recurring revenue programs that are like $5 and under, and that did really well. I didn't expect it to do that. I'm like, "Oh, this will probably be a nice little hit".

In baseball terms, I thought I'd be a nice little double but it ended being a home run. Sort of things like that.

But I'll be honest, and I'm not trying to sound cocky, but I get behind an idea, I'm all in and I'm like, "This thing is going to freaking work." Maybe that's why I've been successful because I have this kind of mentality where… it's funny. Right before this, Seth, I just did a coaching call with a woman who's really smart. She ran an offline business for 10 years and she wants to now teach other people how to create systems.

I told her straight up, I said, "The only thing that's going to stop you is your lack of confidence", because she's like, "Well, do I really have enough material? Why would they listen to me?" That's the only thing.

A lot of people don't succeed, not because they don't know the tactics, not because they don't know the paid traffic or all the stuff you need or how to write a good headline that's compelling, but they lack the confidence to do it. So there you go. I don't know if I answered your question.

Seth: Move forward and pull the trigger and take massive action.

Ryan: Right. Absolutely. When you're doing it online, if you keep it streamlined, there's not a lot of risks. How much does it really cost to put out a digital product?

So as long as you're being lean and being smart with it and putting out something like a good product that doesn't have to have all the bells and whistles, (you can always add that later), then there's not a ton of downside.

Seth: Absolutely. With all of the success you've achieved, what is your biggest challenge now?

Ryan: I'm at the point of my business where do you look to grow it even more and take that next step or you're kind of really happy where you are? It's funny I came across this years ago where I decided to go for it, and I got a big office suite and I hired a bunch of people, but almost immediately I was like, "Man, I'm not happy".

I didn't like living in that kind of structure. It was a little more corporate. It was the office, and I just felt like my creativity, everything was just stifled. I couldn't wait to get out of that lease. I went back to what I love doing, which is building virtual businesses and working from home and working from Starbucks and I just feel much more comfortable.

So that's a challenge now. It's like, do I really try to go big and build up all that stuff or do I just kind of stay? Because I make more than enough money. I mean, how much do you need? We have four kids, I'm doing fine. I think entrepreneurs have to realize there are stages of their business where you have to say, "Okay, where am I? What do I want to do next, and what's the next stage?" You have to be careful not to get too complacent and think you know it all.

It's another big challenge people have. They think they know it all, and they stop learning and they stop trying to grow. Then, pardon my French, the shit hits the fan.

Seth: Absolutely. You've written two "real books with a real publisher" as opposed to self-publishing. Talk a little bit about how those were written and how you got a real bookstore book as opposed to just sell-publishing on Amazon?

Ryan: I've written quite a few books. I had a few that were self-published that are real books. I mean, they weren't sold with local bookstore but they were real, hard-cover self-published books. One was called *The Millionaire Workout,* one was called *Passion to Profits*.

The other ones were books that I co-authored. So I'll be honest with you, it was pretty easy. I knew both of the guys, Mark Joyner who was the one putting together the project for the *Worst Case Scenario Business Guide,* and Dave Ricklin who was doing the *Masters of Marketing.* I knew them. I have relationships. They said, "Do you want to be a part of this?" I said, "Absolutely".

The moral of that story, it's really about your network. Everyone focuses on tactic so much when at the end of the day, the guys who have the most success, the men that were most successful, they just have really deep networks. It sounds old school, but that's everything. The fact that you can have a relationship with somebody, you call them up and they could mail for you is like a big thing.

So stay connected. Stay connected. I have an agent now and we're looking at doing another book that I'm going to write myself that would be a real bookstore book. For that, I tell you, you need an agent. You need a really good agent. My advice is, because I was just behind the scenes for a guy who just published the book with a publisher, you need an agent. Essentially, they want you to do the marketing.

They want to see that you have the big list, that you have a big social media following, and that you can sell books. Otherwise, if they're not going to bring you on or if they do, you're going to basically get a "No" upfront.

I have a friend I just spoke to earlier of the day and he has a big list, probably three, four hundred thousand people, and he's probably going to get a million dollar advance for his first book.

Seth: Wow.

Ryan: Yeah. No matter what, build your list. Build your list. Build your list. Build your list. That's number one. Everything else, even all the other stuffs, social media, all that old stuff, that's fine and good. Facebook owns you. I mean, they could take it away at any time; they can close your account.

If you have this email list, your clients, your subscribers, your customers, that is your most viable asset. So protect that with your life and never stop focusing on building your list. Then from there, then you can go to publishers and get book. Then you could do whatever you want.

Seth: That is excellent advice. You know, you brought up something really interesting. You brought up the fact that if it's on Facebook, Facebook owns it; you don't. They could close your account at any time. We've had that happen multiple times. Are you seeing that Facebook and other source of media sites are becoming a whole lot more restrictive in terms of what you can do on their advertising platforms?

Ryan: Facebook is. Yeah. With one of our supplement companies, we had a lot of issues with our accounts getting closed down. Legit products, legit research, legit science and still closing down. I've said this, and I think I heard this probably first from Dan Kennedy, was the most dangerous number in your business is one.

Seth: Yes.

Ryan: Whether the whole business is just you or whether you're only relying on one marketing tactic. I mean, you'll see some people who have a little bit of success with the traffic on the Facebook and they put all their eggs in that Facebook basket. The minute their account is closed, they're dead. A hundred percent of their revenue is gone.

If you're building up your infrastructure and you've just signed a three-year lease for that 5,000 square-foot space and you just bought your Bentley because you can't wait to show it off on Facebook in front of all your buddies, those payments aren't going away. So you've got to be smart and you've got to always diversify everything. Have backups in place with back-up systems and back-up traffic and constantly look for new ways to not only get new leads, but then obviously you still have to take care of your current customers.

Seth: Good advice. You are also writing a column on entrepreneur magazine. Talk a little bit about that and how that came to pass.

Ray: Yeah. That came to pass, again, it comes back to connections. I saw one of my friends writing for them. I said, "Oh, man, I see you're writing for them. It was always one of my dreams to write for entrepreneur." I said, "Would you mind connecting me?" He said, "Absolutely". Made the email connection. I pitched a few article ideas, wrote a sample. They liked it, and boom, I was in.

This is a person that I've had a relationship with and I've promoted his stuff, he's promoted mine. I've given him support. I'll do free coaching calls for my friends. So it's all give and take. You've just got to spend some time getting away from the computer, picking up the phone, calling people, reaching out, and just trying to be a good person and offering to help instead of emailing me. Every day, "Hey Ron, I got this new product. I'm selling it on Clickbank. It's a 50% commission. Your audience will love it. Can you promote it?" No, I can't.

Someone who takes your time where they buy a coaching session with me or they brought my product and they give me a video testimonial makes me want to help them and help them out. So there's my advice. Just try to do good things.

Seth: What do you find when you were doing coaching calls with people, you'd mention the lack of confidence already, but are you finding is, let's say, some of the most common mistakes people are making that you're helping them with?

Ryan: People that I'm coaching?

Seth: Yes.

Ryan: First thing is they're trying to be too innovative. They're trying to reinvent the wheel. If you're in the fitness market and you see the Top 30 products all have a similar layout, a similar structure, similar pricing, that doesn't mean you should be a cowboy and do something that is so outrageous. These people are already spending time and money to show that something works and it's proven. Just model them.

Now I'm not saying copy, because I can't stand when people do that, but model what they're doing. Model the pricing. Model the structure and just find the way to make yours a little bit better. The advice is find what's working and make it better.

The other thing I find is that people come to me with an idea and it's more about prevention. They're not going to pay for prevention. I did a call last week with a physical therapist and he said, "One of my ideas is doing this whole thing about preventing hamstring injuries". I said, "Well, you're a physical therapist. You've seen 500 clients over the past couple of years. How many clients have ever come to you saying, 'You know what, can I pay you so I could prevent the hamstring injury?" He said, "None". I said, "Of course". So that's one thing.

Related to that is people get way too emotionally attached to their product or their idea. I know they're in trouble when they start off and they say, "I want to sell this. This is something that I love and I want to sell this." Well, it doesn't matter what you want. It's what customers want and what they're willing to pay for.

There's so many mistakes people make. Another mistake is spending way too much time and effort on trying to build this 17 upsells and downsells and spending $20,000 on copywriting for 30 autoresponder sequence when they don't even know if their initial product is going to work. It's all about that initial offer because if your initial offer doesn't work, all the other stuff doesn't matter.

So it's really about creating an offer that is a no-brainer that it's just like, "Yes". The minute people see it, they can't wait to get their wallet up. I'm working on something new now and I just talked to my friend about 3 hours this, the one who's getting that big book deal. I told him the concept, the program we're building, the company, the pricing, and he's like, "I want to buy that right now". Then I go, "Okay, I'm on to something".

So that's it. That's the whole thing. It's not, "Hey, you want to hear about my seven upsells?" So those are some mistakes.

Seth: I appreciate that. What keeps you going when things don't go your way? When they don't work out how you want?

Ryan: I don't know. Maybe because I'm from New York. If we get hit, we just come back. I've always been a fighter. Not like fist fights. I just work best when my backs against the wall. A challenge in overcoming adversity, that really kind of gets me pumped up.

If I'm ever feeling down or had a bad day or something, I'll be honest, I'm just playing with my kids. I look at a picture of my kids and everything's all right. What's the worst that can happen? I guess working for this first six years, as I told you in the children's rehab hospital, I mean, I worked with every kid with every imaginable disease you could imagine. Everything from cancer to things like scleroderma, which is like all the arteries are hardening where this girl would like scream at night because she's like dying. I've seen so many kids die from the worst diseases.

So you see that every single day for six years, you don't really sweat the small stuff. "Okay, that guy didn't promote my product; he said he would. Okay. My kids aren't dying from cancer." So I always try to put things in perspective. On my death bed, am I really going to worry about this? Am I really going to worry about what that person said about me on Facebook or because the product didn't go quite according to expectations? No. I'm not.

So I don't sweat it. I just keep moving my feet and keep moving on. I get excited. Okay, what's the next thing I'm going to do? How am I going to make this even better? Boom, I'm back up.

Seth: You may have just answered this question, but what personality trait would you attribute the majority of your success to?

Ryan: I mean I do think the ability to bounce back is probably much stronger. I don't know. I just have a lot of compassion for people, and I truly want to help, and I hear that all time. Say, "Ryan, I follow some other guys online but I feel like you really care for my success and I feel like you really care about me. You're not full of scam, like I can see you're a real guy". I think that's it, just being just a humble real person.

Stop trying to be sleek and trying to be this crazy nut job. Just be you. If you show that you actually care about them, you're not just there to steal their money, that you're there to actually provide a lot of value, then they'll respond and they'll respond positively. It's just basic social skills.

Seth: So be you, not the crazy nut job. All right.

Ryan: Be you. You can quote me on that.

Seth: I've wrote it down. Who is an ideal client for you?

Ryan: Someone who is really, really passionate. I love passionate people and people who are just persistent and are not going to give up. I love working with people like that. Their focus, it's not just about the money. It's really about making an impact, and they want to truly help people because they are the most fun clients to work with. I remember a couple of years ago when I had people call me and then we will talk. If they were appropriate for it, I would pitch them. I'd say, "Look, I have this coaching. Are you interested?"

One person was saying, "Ryan, I just want to do a 97 a month program." "What topic?" "I don't care. I just want to do a 97 a month". "What is it you do? What do you want to talk about?" "I don't care. I just want to do a 97 a month".

Seth, I swear to you, this was the conversation. I'm like, "Look, I'm not the right guy for you." I'm just not. That was it. That's fine. I'm going to go and find someone else. But those aren't the kind of clients I want to work with.

Seth: I could see how that would be an issue.

Ryan: Yes.

Seth: For our folks who are listening that are resonating with your story and what you're saying, who are that fit, who are passionate, that do you want to help and make a difference and want more from you, where should we send them? What website? What podcast? What social media presence? What book?

Ryan: Just go to ryanlee.com. R-Y-A-N-L-E-E and sign up and do it. I email just about every day with different marketing tips and strategies and advice. We had a little fun. We have a lot of people on there. A lot of the big marketers subscribe to do it. So definitely go to ryanlee.com.

Then also, you can go to my Facebook page, facebook.com/ryanleemarketing. I post on there and I answer questions. So that's it. That's two simple ways.

Seth: Awesome. Okay. It's been a fascinating. I've got pages of note. I greatly appreciate it. With Ryan Lee of ryanlee.com, facebook.com/ryanleecoaching. Thank you so much for participating.

Ryan: It's my please. Thanks for having me, Seth.

INTERVIEW WITH
TIM ROMERO

Seth: Today, I have the great fortune to be interviewing Tim Romero.

Tim: Thanks so much for having me.

Seth: Well, we really appreciate it. It is an honor for our listeners to get to hear from someone like you. Can you tell us a little bit about what you're doing and the amazing stuff you're doing with your podcast? I know we'd love to hear about it.

Tim: Okay. Well, I try to keep it brief. About 20 years ago, I found myself in Japan. I started four companies here. I've sold two. I bankrupted two. So I'm batting 500.

Seth: Did that get you in the Hall of Fame?

Tim: Yeah. These days, it's a pretty good record. But Japan right now is going through this amazing transformation. There really is a sort of birth of entrepreneurship here. And I've been very plugged in the scene as you might imagine for the last 20 years. Last September I started a podcast in English called Disrupting Japan where I'm trying to introduce Japanese startup founders to the rest of the world. And it's just really taken off in a way that I never expected both domestically here in Japan and internationally as well.

Seth: That's great. You said it took off in a way you never expected. Obviously, I'm assuming you started with zero. Where are you at the time of this interview?

Tim: We all start with zero. About 2000 listeners per episode.

Tim: You can't get more niche than this particular market. I mean, to introduce Japanese startups to the rest of the world, it's a very small niche.

Seth: I would imagine.

Tim: It happens to be my niche.

Seth: Yes. That's all that matter. It's not making yourself famous to people at Starbucks but making yourself famous to your target market.

Tim: Exactly.

Seth: I know a lot of podcasters have these misconceptions or myths when they start. How do you select and find the great guests that you have on your show?

Tim: So, selecting is actually different. I'm not looking for sponsorship so I guess I have a whole lot more freedom than most people do. Podcasting is an incredible intimate media. I mean, most people are listening to it on their headphones. We are literally whispering in people's ears right now.

Seth: I never thought about it like that. That's a very terrific way to put it.

Tim: I try to find people who have good stories to tell. So facing the rest of the world, I'm trying to find people who are showing

Americans and Europeans that Japanese founders are not the salary men, that they're creative, innovative people just like entrepreneurs everywhere. Social entrepreneurship is only now becoming acceptable here. And I'm showing the Japanese that look, the startup founders are not some kind of special exotic creatures. They are people like you and me. They just decided to take a couple of chances. And just finding people with great stories really gets across both ways. And so some of the guys are post IPO, some are just starting out but they just have all amazing stories to tell.

Seth: It's all about the story.

Tim: It really is.

Seth: What do you wish you knew when you started that you know now?

Tim: How unimportant the audio quality and all the technical things are. It's not going to make or break the podcast. I wish I understood it first that really it's about connecting with people much more so than any technology or any kind of promotion. It's more storytelling than marketing. It took me a while for that to sink in.

Seth: That's a great lesson. I know that just like your Japanese entrepreneurs and yourself batting 500, sometimes we learn more from our failures than our successes. What has been your biggest mistake? And what did you learn from it?

Tim: In podcast or my entrepreneurial life?

Seth: Let's do both. Let's do podcast first and then entrepreneurial life because I'd be curious on that too.

Tim: Okay. With the podcast, I think my biggest mistake was trying to make it seem like I was more like a radio-type person rather than just a normal person talking to other people.

When I kind of dropped that façade and just started having conversations, things just turned around immediately.

Seth: Wow. So a definite mindset shift right there.

Tim: Yeah. It is. I guess the shift is like you're not trying to impress anybody. You're trying to talk to people. And that was my biggest mistake early on. It was trying to sound like someone on the radio. My biggest mistake entrepreneurial-wise, it is my second company. I turned over sales to somebody else because I'm a programmer at heart. Never do that. Never turn over sales to someone else until you really understand what your process is, until you understand every step and can diagram it. And that company failed largely because of that.

Seth: And yet, here you are four companies later, two successful and you survived.

Tim: Well, I'm pretty much unemployable.

Seth: I resemble that remark.

Tim: People doing startups it's – I'll talk to people who are like "we really need out-of-the-box thinkers". You think you do but you don't really. So they're more people that can stay within your box but be creative.

Seth: Interesting. I love that you're being open and transparent because a lot of folks won't talk about what went wrong. They want to cover it up. And I've been guilty of that. I've had issues over the years where I didn't want to air the dirty laundry. And it's only been I'd say the last 6-12 months when I've really been working on to make my mess my message. People need to know that it isn't all wine and roses and that there are tremendous ups and downs. So you don't have to go into specifics about the businesses that went bankrupt. But how did you emotionally cope with that? How did you get through to the other side? Talk a little bit about the bad if you're open to doing that.

Tim: Sure, sure. Well, how I coped with it, not well quite frankly.

Seth: That's a real answer.

Tim: I wish I could say I just realized that you focus where you want to go and you keep going and I eventually kind of got to that point. But no, it's really hard. You pour a lot of yourself into what you're building whether you're building a company or a podcast or a band I suppose. And when it falls apart, if it doesn't hurt, you weren't really that into it I suppose.

Seth: That's it. That's a writer downer folks.

Tim: I wish I knew a shortcut I could tell you to make it easier but you just kind of suffer through it. You come out the other side and you do it again.

Seth: What is your biggest challenge now?

Tim: Finding a single project that I'm excited enough to dedicate 90% of my time to. I'm in the envied position that I've got amazing contacts. I'm advising a lot of different startups and investing in a bunch of startups. There's this wonderful passion and excitement that comes when you can really like sink your teeth into something and say yeah, this is why I'm out, this is what I'm staying up late, getting up early to do. My biggest challenge right now is finding that.

Seth: Interesting. You had mentioned earlier about all of the reading and research that you do and the consuming of everything you can find on the topic and the thing that you're passionate about. What are the three best books you've ever read that had the most impact on your work? And you're not allowed to reference either the Bible or a book you wrote yourself.

Tim: Fair enough. Before I answer, I'll say these are books that profoundly affected me. A lot of them, they just kind of found me at the right point in my life. So I'm not necessarily recommending this to everyone but they had a huge impact on me. I would say Tony Robbins' *Awaken the Giant Within* which is just a fantastic book.

Seth: Absolutely.

Tim: It's amazing how well it holds up. Zig Ziglar's *Ziglar on Selling* and I think that deserves a little bit of background because when you start as an engineer, you develop this healthy mistrust of salesmen, right?

Seth: Yes.

Tim: Sales seems something that's somehow, I don't know, immoral or sleazy. Ziglar's book really reframed it. He was saying that if you believe in what you're selling, you are doing your customer a service. Your job is to help your customer get over the fear of investing in you and believing in you.

Seth: This is another writer downer.

Tim: That book, it totally transformed my way of thinking about sales and business and that not only could a great salesman have integrity but a great salesman must have integrity. So that book fundamentally changed my thinking.

Seth: You're two for two. What's number three?

Tim: A little book called *As a Man Thinketh*.

Seth: Another great book.

Tim: You've read it. That's great!

Seth: I've read all three. If I had a webcam in your office and took a picture of your bookshelf, I guarantee that the one behind me has no books on Japan on it. So I'm stopping there but I have a feeling we have a lot of the same business, marketing, personal development and spiritual books on our shelves.

Tim: One thing I have noticed is that if you really – there's been these phases of self-help and development to *As A Man*

Thinketh. That was written around 1900, before 1900. Wasn't it?

Seth: It's a really old book. Yeah.

Tim: So that book, it really becoming the best person you can be and cultivating your mind and helping you focus on the wonderful things in life, on positivity. And then, it went through sort of Napoleon Hill like how to be successful. And I think there's something that's more fundamentally true with the old ones that aren't so much about how to get what you want and they're more about how to be a better person.

Seth: That makes sense.

Tim: It ultimately helps you get what you want.

Seth: Right, of course. Who you are affects how well what you do works.

Tim: Absolutely.

Seth: For our listeners who are resonating with your story, who want to learn more about what you're doing, again the name of the podcast for them to subscribe to and websites for them to go to, books that are – how else can they see more of Tim?

Tim: Okay. The podcast is disruptingjapan.com. I have a blog as well at t3.org but right now the podcast is really my application. I'm putting a lot of effort into that. So please check it out, subscribe. If you're in Tokyo, if you ever find yourself here, there's actually a resource at that site that is like the best way to get plugged in to the startup community here. And there are a lot of meet up events. And if any of your listeners are in town, shoot me some email. I'll introduce you around.

Seth: That is very nice of you. Again, this has been Seth Greene interviewing Tim Romero of disruptingjapan.com. Tim, thank you again so much for joining us.

Tim: Delighted to be here.

INTERVIEW WITH
NARESH VISSA

Seth: Can you tell us a little bit about what you have got going on and what you're doing? Because you are up to some pretty interesting stuff.

Naresh: So I am an online marketer with a focus on the financial space. You can call me online marketer, you can call me a publisher of information but really my focus is on two main areas. The first area is the publishing of financial research. And so I have a startup called Moneyball Economics where we provide statistical research and analysis on publicly traded companies and also on the broader economy as a whole. And I'm the publisher of that so I basically manage the business. And the other area that I'm involved in is really the nitty gritty of online marketing. So as you know, online marketing is a broad field, There's so much that goes into it and my small business, Krish Media and Marketing, services various clients to help them improve their sales or increase their sales in the online marketing space.

Now, the reason I think that your listeners and you would be interested in hearing from me today is because I'm also an author. I'm not only a publisher but I'm a writer and an author and I released a book about six months ago called *Podcastnomic: The Book of Podcasting to Make You Millions*. And it's all about digital media and podcasting, why people should podcast, how to set up your podcast, how lucrative podcasting can be. And it's essentially a blueprint that provides individuals with everything they need to know about podcasting from soup to nuts.

Seth: That is exactly why we should be listening to you. I love it. How did you get started in podcasting? How did you go from "the publishing" you were doing to the wonderful world of iTunes?

Naresh: So I actually got started in the terrestrial radio space. I'm a former reporter. I went to journalism school for my undergrad years. This was back when radio was still a major medium of content consumption. So this was pre-recession, pre-2008 when the economy went down the gutter but I started out in terrestrial radio. And that's when I realized while working there that radio was dying. It wasn't even a slow death. It was a pretty rapid death. And the recession, the great recession of 2008 expedited that death. So a handful of these big radio communication companies started buying up the smaller players and now there's been so much consolidation that the terrestrial radio space is really, really, really struggling now.

So while I was working in terrestrial radio, I started worrying for my future. I started thinking well, there is no future in radio, there's no future in old school print journalism, newspapers, magazines. And that was kind of my introduction in podcasting because more and more people at the turn of the century were getting their information from the internet whether it was print news information or even audio and video content. They were going online to get it. So that's where podcasting entered because the greatness of podcasting is podcasters have a platform to disseminate their content. Just like authors have a platform in Amazon to disseminate their work, podcasters have iTunes to disseminate their work. And there are now, by the end of this year, there are going to be more than a billion people using an IOS device whether it's an iPhone or an iPad or a Mac computer, laptop. Whatever it might be, there are going to be more than a billion people using it. And with the new IOS updates, the podcast app is automatically ingrained. It automatically comes with all these IOS devices. So as a podcaster, there are now close to a billion people who have access to the podcast app which means it's much easier for them to find you and to start listening to you. So all of this kind of led to the death of radio and really jump started a brand new industry in podcasting.

Seth: I would agree. And that billion number is only going to grow. We heard from another guest on my show that had good reason to know that now they're going to bundle the Apple interface and the iTunes and podcast app into automobiles as the new versions start coming out. So within let's say five years of everyone's hypothetical car turning over, you've got all of those people who might not have an IOS device but now they're going to get one by default with their cars. So it makes the market even bigger.

Naresh: Oh, absolutely. It's only going to continue to get bigger. Not everyone right now has a smartphone, not everyone right now has Bluetooth capabilities in their cars but the smartphone is rapidly, rapidly adapting within the United States and globally so it's almost ubiquitous to have a smartphone now. All of this is just going to take away from terrestrial and FM radio and it's going to bring to the forefront apps like Pandora, Spotify and then of course podcasts so people can listen to them during their drives.

Seth: Absolutely. What do you wish you knew when you started that you know now?

Naresh: It's very, very difficult to make money in terrestrial radio because you're so dependent on advertising as your primary revenue driver. And so as a result, I didn't really get a good business education in the media space. But once I started learning about podcasting where as a podcaster you have control not just over you message but you have control over how you make money, the revenue drivers, the revenue channels started to open up. No longer do you have to solely depend on advertising but with podcasts, you can also come up with premium podcasts, meaning you charge people to listen to special podcasting content. And there are hosting providers like Libsyn and also through iTunes where you can create a pay wall or you can create your own pay wall and it will sit on your own website that you can come up with premium content and charge.

You can also sell an existing product that you might have. So if you're an author and you have a couple of books, you can sell your books. If you're an accountant and you are looking for more clients, you can sell your accounting services. You can do all this through podcasting. And so I actually entered the podcasting space solely because this is where things were shifting. I noticed that the media was shifting towards this more digital landscape. But what I didn't realize early on was you could actually make a lot of money through podcasting and that was really the genesis of the book that I wrote *Podcastnomics* because a lot of people look at podcasting as a hobby or as a fun thing to do. But I've had more than 25 different clients in the radio and podcasting industry and I've seen firsthand how lucrative podcasting can be for a podcaster in his or her business.

Seth: You've grown tremendously. You're very, very successful. You've got a broad base. You've got a million balls in the air. What's your biggest challenge?

Naresh: Well, one of the issues that small businesses have to deal with in any given industry is the downturn. There are certain sectors within the financial space that go through downturns even when the broader economy is up. So for example, a couple of years ago, my biggest client was a company that sold gold. And it was difficult because the price of gold has plummeted over the past three to four years. It's just absolutely plummeted. And so during those times even though the broader economy is doing well, things can get very difficult because margin isn't where it needs to be. So that's one of the challenges that most business people have to deal with regardless of the industry.

But the other challenge is – I'm really more of a business startup type of guy. I enjoy creating things rather than working with a client or working for someone. And as you probably noticed, Seth, when you're out on your own and trying to create value, trying to create a new product or create a new service, you go through your ups and downs not just with the development of the business and the product but there are all sorts of things that pop up, legal issues, macroeconomic issue, things that you can't really plan. And so those are really the downs that not many people hear about when they talk to an entrepreneur. It gets very, very bumpy.

Seth: Absolutely. It's funny that you mentioned that because people ask me, "How's it going? What's going on? What's new?" And depending on the day, you're either on top of the world and everything is going great and the highs are super high but the lows are also super low. It's a rollercoaster. I was meeting with a magazine publisher the other day. And we were talking about this very issue. And he said, "I tell people the great news is I own a business and the really bad news is I own a business." So you are absolutely right. And I was speaking at a Speaking Empire event last year and one of the other speakers, a woman named Ferlie Almonte, had an amazing quote that I wrote down when she was telling her story. And she said, "If your why doesn't make you cry, it's not strong enough." And the other thing she said that really resonated with me is she said, "Make your mess your message." So that's my seventh book. It's going to be – because my first five were all on business. My sixth is on podcasting. My seventh is going to be my story of the struggle because I think that helps people realize they're not alone. Everybody doesn't go from zero to a million overnight. And there is an incredible amount of challenges and stress. And to normalize that I think will probably – if it helps one person, then obviously it's worth it.

Naresh: Oh, absolutely.

Seth: The perfect segue. I know you are a voracious learner. What are three of the best books you've ever read that had the most impact on your work? And you can't quote the Bible or a book you wrote.

Naresh: This is a great question. Now, I am a voracious reader and listener. So when I say listener, I listen to a lot of podcasts which I think is really the – podcasts and audio books are great new ways to consume content. But to answer your question head on, one of the books that I think prepared me and my mindset or gave me a framework to really pursue business and to also tackle many facets of life is *Seven Habits of Highly Effective People* by Stephen Covey. There are some take-aways from that book that are actually life changing. So for example, Covey talked about four areas that people should implement in their life because he himself did it and saw improvement. And those four areas were really kind of physically staying in shape, mentally being around people who you're okay with, spiritually giving thanks to the world (not necessarily being religious – I am a bit religious but I consider myself more spiritual which is really more about giving thanks and being happy for the way your life is) – and mentally exercising your brain to stay sharp.

And he mentioned these four things are that I found to be pretty life changing, that I myself have implemented in my own life. And I know many other people have talked about him. James Altucher who you might have had on your show before, he kind of took Covey's idea and called it a daily practice of mental, spiritual, physical and emotional health. Almost like a four-legged stool, you need all four legs. You can't have three because if you have three, then the stool is going to fall. And so I really, really like that book a lot.

The other book that has made a big impact on me was actually James Altucher's book. He came out with about two years ago called *Choose Yourself.* And the book wasn't really anything new but the way Altucher wrote it it's all about how the economy is changing drastically in every way is possible. Industries are changing. They're slashing workers. Full-time jobs are going down. Outsourcing is going up. And so a lot of people would look at this and say "hey, this is a bad thing, this is bad for our economy." But I think the truly introspective person will take a look at it and say "this is actually an opportunity, this is my chance to start my own business and to contract out my services because I come cheaper than a full-time employee or this is my chance to go out on my own and do my own thing because I can't depend on the corporate world anymore." So that was a big take-away that I got from *Choose Yourself* which was James Altucher's book.

And then the other book that has really affected me in the way I live my life is or actually there are several but Malcolm Gladwell, his several books, *Outliers, The Tipping Point, Blink* – I can kind of couple all of them together but Gladwell is a great storyteller. And the ideas that he writes about are fully backed up by anecdotal and quantitative research.

Seth: Those are awesome recommendations. That is very helpful for our folks. For the listeners who are resonating with what you're saying and want to learn more about all the different things you have to offer, I know you have obviously so many different things going on, what podcast of yours should they subscribe to? What website should they go to? Plug the book please again so that they can go get it.

Naresh: Yeah. I greatly appreciate it. So the book is called *Podcastnomics.* It's available on Amazon in audio book, Kindle and paper back so all versions are available. If you want to subscribe for my free newsletter, you can visit the Podcastnomics official website which is www.podcastnomics.com. And there are also links on that website to buy the book as well. But yeah, you can buy the book, *Podcastnomics,* and get the free newsletter at podcastnomics.com. And at podcastnomics.com, there's also an email address for you to contact me if you have any questions, just want to say hi or interested in any of my marketing, online marketing or project management services.

Seth: Okay. Awesome. We greatly appreciate it. This has been Seth Greene interviewing Naresh Vissa. Thank you so much for joining us. It's been an honor to have you on the show.

Naresh: Thanks so much, Seth. It's been an honor to be interviewed by you.

Seth: I greatly appreciate it.

INTERVIEW WITH
VICKENS MOSCOVA

Seth: I'm here today joined by Vickens Muscova. Vickens, welcome.

Vickens: All right. Thanks so much for having me. My pleasure.

Seth: We greatly appreciate it. I'm going to have to go back in time for a minute and ask you how you got started.

Vickens: Well, I realized a while ago when I was promoting clubs, in Manhattan, that I needed to do something that was a bit more substantial with these brands and businesses. So what I did was I started actually marketing them more professionally using social media and all the different types of marketing that are coming out today to really build these brands. And then the people that were actually at the event started contacting me to see if I could help them with their companies. So that's how I started.

Seth: And how did you go from there to what you're doing now?

Vickens: Well, just consistent work. Social media definitely has a big hand to do with that but really just keeping it consistent and really studying every day and understanding what's coming out in the future and then applying that to my current clients.

Seth: Okay. How did you get involved in podcasting?

Vickens: Well, because of content marketing, I realized that inbound marketing was going to become bigger and I needed to use more different kinds of platforms to put myself out there in a way that was valuable in providing information and content. So I got into podcasting. And I've met a lot of interesting people so I wanted to interview them. So in interviewing them, it started to take a life on its own and I just kept it going.

Seth: And if you look back, what do you wish you knew when you started that you know now?

Vickens: That family and friends were probably going to be the last people to support me. So I wish when I started out I wasn't looking towards them for help and I just went to like-minded individuals that were ready to work. So that's what I would do different.

Seth: That makes total sense. I could certainly resemble that remark. Who are the ideal guests for your podcast now?

Vickens: Well, my ideal guest would be a business owner, somebody that wants to expand using marketing and wants to really build their brand. Right now because – I don't really have subscribers on it because it's on Blog Talk Radio but I do have people that follow it.

Seth: And with all you've got going on, I know that you've got a lot of irons in different fires so to speak, what is your biggest challenge day to day now?

Vickens: Biggest challenge day to day would probably be I guess finding new work to do. Once you have the work, it's just really easy to do and keep going and moving. And that takes a lot of time from what you're doing. So I have to develop a way to make it easier on myself so I don't have difficulties in finding fresh new work to do to keep myself busy and entertained.

Seth: I can certainly understand that. I know you use a bunch of different techniques to help those brands that you're working with. Without naming any names to protect your clients' confidentiality, can you tell me someone that you worked recently with? You can call them Mr. and Mrs. Jones or whatever you want or ABC Incorporated. Tell me about a recent client and what they were looking for and a great case study of what you're able to do for them.

Vickens: Well, most recently, I was working with a PR company that really wanted to understand how to use marketing and social media. So what I had to do was actually come on board and reinvent the whole social media marketing strategy and to provide a sound way to make it so that they're not all about me, me, me. One of the clients they're representing was a hotel chain. And I saw right away that the engagement was pretty low because they were consistently just putting out basically ads using the social platforms without really engaging and getting to know the potential clients I saw an opportunity there. So I have to build the engagement, grow it a bit faster and organically.

Seth: That makes total sense. If you don't mind and using estimates, what type of results were you able to get in that growth? And how was that perceived by your client?

Vickens: Well, the thing when you're working with a corporate company, they really just want to see how that work is going to help their bottom line and return on investments. So they were pretty happy that the engagement went up because that means that more people are talking about the brand.

Seth: Absolutely. What is then one of your most successful campaigns for a client?

Vickens: One of my most successful campaigns – because I actually build brands online, one of my most successful clients – I was working with this guy that worked for the EPA that just wanted to create a new home-based business. So I felt really proud that I was able to actually take his idea from nothing to something and create a new income stream for his family. So I was really proud about that.

Seth: As you should be. That's great. That sounds like you made a huge difference not just in his business but I'm sure that it affected his life positively as well.

Vickens: Oh yeah.

Seth: With all this going on – and I mean, we've got constant change. It seems like there's a new social network every couple of weeks, there's a new app, there's always something changing. How do you stay on the cutting edge?

Vickens: I stay on the cutting edge by not waiting until something new comes out. I actually study in advance by really going in deep with the companies that are the ones that are creating the platforms and tools. So, I attend a lot of events where these people are speaking and then I get a chance to just talk to them one on one so in that way I can really be in the forefront of the innovation.

Seth: A way to keep your finger ahead of the pulse almost. What magazines, trade journals, newsletters, what do you read every month?

Vickens: Business News Wire, Mashable, all the different types of social media. There's a Social Media Examiner. I'm on jointerest. com which I also contribute to. So I like a different array of different kinds of publication that speak on the marketing aspects while also going into technology.

Seth: What are three of the best books you've ever read that had the most impact on your work? And you can't quote the Bible or a book you wrote.

Vickens: The *Art of Seduction* was pretty good.

Seth: By Robert Greene. It's a great book.

Vickens: Right. And then he wrote one with 50 Cent that I really like.

Seth: *50th Law.* Yeah, that was an awesome book.

Vickens: Right. And then Russell Simmons also had a book that came out not too long ago where he was speaking on the law of attraction and different spiritual aspects that Oprah brought to the forefront with Eckhart Tolle's *A New Earth*. So I'm in to all these different types of books that help you work on yourself from the inside out. And when you do that, you can apply it to your daily life and habits and business.

Seth: I love that. That's a great answer. With all of the companies out there that are purporting to do some of what you do and help brands grow, how do you differentiate yourself?

Vickens: I differentiate myself by understanding that professionalism is key while at the same time just doing things a bit differently. (Whether it be how I post something, how I hashtag it.) Just to create my own style and stick with it but making sure that that style is engaging and builds the brands and also is very useful by using the different platforms of high quality. I use

Facebook or Twitter and I find what's the most powerful aspect of it and then I apply that to what I do while other people don't do that. I mean they just really use it when they need it. I kind of integrated all the most powerful aspects of social media into what I do daily. And one aspect was that we spoke about a bit earlier was the podcasting.

Seth: Yes. And for folks who are listening who want more, who are resonating with the things that you're saying and want to learn more about you and what you're doing, where is the best place for us to send them to? Do you want them to go to a website? Do you want them to go to Blog Talk Radio and subscribe to you? What is the first step for them to take?

Vickens: First, I would actually just email or call me. My number is 848-628-4873. And then my personal email is vickensm@gmail.com. And then I have a personal website as well, vickensmoscova.com. And from that contact sheet, it goes directly to my email. And then also, I have a couple of different blogs. If you go to vmenterprises.wordpress.com, you could take a look at some of the work I've done with social media. My portfolio is actually on vickensmoscova.com and you can check out some results from some work, past work I've done. So it's been pretty good. So people could reach me like everywhere. Especially if you just Google me, I'll pop up with all these different articles from AP, Fox, everything.

Seth: All right. Well, we will send them there. Thanks so much for doing the interview.

Vickens: Thank you so much. I really appreciate it. Keep up the great work.

Seth: Thank you.

INTERVIEW WITH
DAVE SWERDLICK

Seth: Welcome to Direct Response Marketing Magic. I am your host, Seth Greene. I have the good fortune today of interviewing Dave Swerdlick. Dave, welcome to the show. Thanks for doing the interview.

Dave: Hey. Well, thanks for having me, Seth. I very much appreciate it.

Seth: Not a problem. My pleasure. Let's take you back in time a little bit and ask you how you got started.

Dave: Started in podcasting?

Seth: Yes.

Dave: I got started – you know, it really was kind of a fluke. I bought a Mac computer in 2007. My past career is I had been in radio station in Colorado. I found out how easy GarageBand is to work, you know, on a Mac. And I had a couple – they were small children at that time and I said, "How about for a family project, why don't we do a podcast?" And of course they said, "What's a podcast?"

Seth: Right.

Dave: I said, "Don't worry about it but you can pick any subject you want. We're going to do it. We're going to talk about any subject you want." So they – we had just gotten back from Chicago. We made the pilgrimage to the American Girl Doll Store and they were so into the American Girl dolls. I said, "Okay, no problem." I said, "But we have to do it next week." So when next week came around, they changed their mind and they wanted to do it with Webkinz. Are you familiar Webkinz?

Seth: Yes. I have three little kids.

Dave: Oh, perfect. Okay. So we started something called the Webkinz Webcast in 2007 and it just so – and again, my kids can pick any subject they wanted because it's just a fun family project. It just so happened that year, it was in 2007 or 2008, Webkinz was the most searched term on Google. So everyone was in the Webkinz and we just got a ton of viewers. We're doing it audio only at that time. We had the Webkinz Webcast and we gave the latest news about these stuffed animals and upcoming ones. And the kids had a lot of fun with it. So, you know, in our hometown here, we were on the front page of the paper. I think that got picked up by national media, Washington Post and Seattle Times.

It was fun because we read listener's email from literally around the world, Hong Kong to Tibet, to the Philippines. People would write in and we would read all of that. And the kids had a lot of fun. So the kids grew up and they were not into Webkinz anymore. So we started a different podcast. But anyway, that's how we got started in podcasting literally as a family project. Because of my background in radio, I kind of kept the conversation rolling along and they loved it.

Seth: That's incredible. Funny that it turned into a family business almost. My wife writes a blog called whinypaluza.com about her hilarious adventures as a stay-at-home mom of three very active little kids and they do toy review videos on YouTube with Amazon affiliate links next to the ones they thought were good. And then they'd be honest and say. Dad bought this toy for us. We played with it for a week and then never touched it again so don't buy it. And now, they get a check from Amazon. And they're the world's youngest affiliate marketers and they got written about in a couple of small business magazines. Every week, they want to do more videos and ask what's going on. And they've tasked their mommy to write more articles so they get more traffic. It's adorable. I love it.

Dave: That's fantastic. Yeah. At the time when my kids were younger – now, they're 14 and my oldest is going to turn 17 in a couple of weeks and they're fashionistas. So they like money. When they grew out of this Webkinz thing, I was like, "Do you guys still want to do something?" Because they weren't interested so much in Webkinz anymore. And they said, 'Yeah, yeah. We're still on the fun." So we started another podcast called Kid Friday. And if you go into the iTunes podcasts or whatever and look under Kids and Family, you'll usually see Kid Friday on the top 10. And Kid Friday is kind of a tech show for tweens and teens. The episode we just put out recently was a lot of it was about the Apple watch. We also have app recommendations, website recommendations, whatever. But if you search the term app in the iTunes store and then scroll down and look under the podcast area, you'll see Kid Friday listed number two.

Seth: Wow.

Dave: Because of that, we have been getting some advertising and so they love it when Dad gives them a crisp –$100 bill each. So we have Sea World as a sponsor this past month we've done some stuff for apps and things like that. And again, this is still meant to be a family project which it is. So we do video but it's been a lot of fun but it's even more fun when they make money.

Seth: Absolutely. I would agree 100 percent. What do you wish you knew when you started that you know now?

Dave: I knew nothing. I didn't know what a feed was. I didn't know how to get a feed together. I didn't know about where to host, how that works, how hosting works, how anything works. Furthermore, I think podcasting at least on iTunes had been around since like 2006 I think, right? So we got involved in 2007 which was pretty early on. So there wasn't a lot of infrastructure. The recording part was very easy and editing and all that but what to do with it – how do you get it to your listeners? How do you get it to people? And I never thought YouTube would be as big as it is now. I always thought iTunes would be the primary driver. Although some of the Kid Friday stuff is available on YouTube, we never really worked YouTube. So it's a big mistake. I guess I wish I would've known that now as opposed to then and really utilizing YouTube because we really haven't to the extent that we should be.

Seth: My kids are on YouTube, all three of them, eight, six and two. And they're on YouTube all the time. And one of the channels they love is EvanTube and they love him even more because he makes several million dollars a year. And they're like, "Daddy, we need more views. Daddy, we need more views. Can you run some ads for us?" So I totally understand and agree with that. What is your biggest challenge now?

Dave: Well, my biggest challenge now is actually in starting a family project with my kids. It's turned into a full-time business for me. I use iTunes podcasts to see what kind of reaction we get and kind of a proof of concept. So right now, I have a company called StoryCub. And what we do is we work with publishers and authors of children's picture books and create video versions of them for digital It's about making story time anytime. So I think about a kindergarten class. If it's story time, I volunteer. One of my kids is in kindergarten. She said if it's story time, everyone will run across the room and sit down, try to get the best seat and everything.

So what we're doing is we're trying to kind of take that experience and make it available 24/7. So it's just story time. There are no words. We're not an eBook. There are no words highlighted. As a matter of fact, we require the text to be removed from the images, the illustrations because when you have story time, you're not teaching a child necessarily to read especially preschool kids. You're just reading a story, showing them pictures. And we've gone number one on iTunes in the Kids and Family section beating Sesame Street, Nick Jr., some of those. iTunes, it's just been a really good place to test things out. YouTube, would be the mistake that I go back to saying that I probably should be doing more of.

Seth: I agree. We should all be doing more of it. I know from following you that you are a voracious learner and you're always trying to stay on top of everything that's constantly changing and the trends that are going on obviously making the transition from American Girl Dolls to Webkinz and then past that as your kids change in age. How do you stay on top of everything? I mean it seems like constant change. How do you stay on the cutting edge?

Dave: Well, I mean like for StoryCub I saw – because of the previous things I do with the kids, I really have been studying the Kids and Family section in iTunes for years. And I have this idea for StoryCub but I just didn't think the bandwidth was there. I mean there are audio books but there's not, there wasn't any real video story time. So I just constantly every week – because you also like to check and see where you are on the charts and kind of compare it to what you're seeing. But we've had millions of downloads in 216 countries of StoryCub from the podcast alone. So it was a study kind of just looking at the chart and kind of seeing an opening that I felt that parents of preschool aged kids would enjoy. And now I'm still, I'm always picking on it. There's always something new. I'm by no means an expert but I do, I think the charts really help see what's going on, what's working and what's not working.

Seth: I greatly appreciate you taking the time to do the interview. I know how busy you are and how successful you are. Let me ask you this for our listeners who are resonating, who are in your target market or who want to watch the way that you've built an amazing following, where should we send them? Which podcast do you want them to subscribe to? What apps do you want them to download? What website do you want them to go to?

Dave: So you can go to KidFriday.com or you can just search Kid Friday in the podcast. And I know the audio version is also available in a couple of places including, I believe – what's the radio app? I forget. But most people watch on video.

You'll hear us talk about stuff that's totally random, that's just off the wall for kids. And then StoryCub, you can look for StoryCub on iTunes in the podcast or you can go to storycub. com and sign up for the free story of the day. So we put out a free featured video picture book of the day that parents can access for free. Sign up and you get a featured book each day which has a lot of fun and kids are really, really loving it. So storycub.com, kidfriday.com or in iTunes in the podcast.

Seth: Okay. Well, thank you so much. I greatly appreciate the opportunity to interview you for our listeners and we really appreciate it. Thank you so much.

Dave: Absolutely. And you know, I just want to finally say that I think that we kind of fell into some monetization things and I actually started a business because of doing podcasts, an entire business because of it. But, you know, I think there's a niche for everyone. And, you know, like I mentioned, Sea World came out with a host of apps specifically for kids and Sea World kids and they found us. We didn't find them. And so no matter what you're doing, there is an audience out there and there's someone who wants to promote their product.

Seth: Very true.

Dave: So there you go. Thank you again.

Seth: Thanks again. We really appreciate it.

Dave: Thanks.

INTERVIEW WITH
CHRIS CHRISTENSON

Chris: The first episode came out in July 2005. So right after podcasting really got started, I sort of listened to some of the first podcasts out there. Probably the first one I heard was the TWIT podcast in tech with Leo Laporte, and decided that I wanted to podcast. So I started thinking about what did I want to do. I thought about doing a tech podcast. I thought about a religious podcast, which I actually do a lot now, but we had a bunch of friends come over for Memorial Day picnic, and all the best stories were travel stories. Truly a month later, we launched Amateur Traveler.

Seth: How have you grown such a large fan base since obviously it helps getting on the ground floor, but for those of our listeners who...

Chris: It helps to have ten years. There's a lot of things we did not have going forth 10 years ago. The one thing to be clear on is I remember eight months into it being just ecstatic that I was getting 200 people downloading a single episode. Of course, it's easier to get that today because we didn't have merely as many people who knew what a podcast was. We didn't have New and Noteworthy, we didn't have just ways that you could show up and get your word out. We had no social media to speak of that you could promote things. The way it was for me was really just grinding out podcast week after week, day after day, year after year. It took me probably about six years to get to the point where I can get a million downloads a year. It was get PR where you can, I guess, list it in a couple of magazines that basically didn't lead to a whole lot of immediate bumps. We got featured in iTunes a number of times now. That has made a big help, including on the top of the podcast page. Even with that, you have people sampling your podcast. You'll get a lot of people who listen to one…

Seth: Right.

Chris: …and they may or may not listen to it again because it really just depends on: one, if they are good; two, is it what they are looking for? For some yes, for some no. Time and persistence.

Then I also do a lot of promotion. Every time I put out the show, it's been about an hour at least, an hour to two hours doing promotion. I will write every tourism board, for instance, that we talk about their destination, the person who's the guest, give them a player that they could put on website. A lot of people who I've had on a show have an audience, so that's going to help.

Some of them will do additional promotion because I'm trying to help them, although you'd be surprised the number who just really don't have a clue and they've got this free piece of content that they should be getting out on their mailing list and they should be telling people about because I'm telling people they should go to the destination and they don't, but some do.

Seth: The tourism board, obviously everyone I would hope, would know to have the guest promote that they were on the show.

Chris: Right.

Seth: But the tourism board, that's a great guerilla marketing strategy. I never would have thought of that. Brilliant. I love it.

Chris: Yeah. I did a chapter... actually, Paul Colligan got a new book out on how to podcast 2015.

Seth: Yup. Paul and Mike are friends of mine.

Chris: Yeah. Paul actually sent the very first podcast expo in 2005, that's when we met. We had basically a meet-up at that podcast expo about making money with your podcast, with me and Paul. Nobody else wanted to think about it apparently at that time. Of course, he's probably made more money than I am, so he's a person I used to look to. I get a thing in his book about promotion and talked about that.

Also he's sudden done a podcast about comics, for instance, and talked about how we could use that same sort of thing with him. So if he does a particular episode for instance, that mentioned the movie that it was done as a comic first and they talk about the comic, then they out to be using the hashtags or the Twitter and hashtag movie and push that out or the fan could enter to use it. Basically, it's who else will benefit from knowing that you just did this great content? Who else did you promote, for instance, who might appreciate it? It might be that we mentioned the actor that was in Captain America, for instance, as part of the podcast, talking about how great he did of rendering this to develop comics.

Seth: Right.

Chris: Give them the mention. "Hey, we mentioned you" or whatever. It's a crack shoot but that can lead to some additional promotion.

Seth: Always be promoting.

Seth: You're in a very crowded space. How do you differentiate yourself from the now hundreds of podcast on your topic, if not thousands?

Chris: I am actually not in a very crowded space. Interestingly enough, I've seen a lot of travel podcasts come and go as you can imagine in 10 years. The interesting thing is, I've outlasted almost all of the companies that have come in. A lot of companies came in, say, 2006, 2007 and dropped out. So Lonely Planet, New York Times travel used to have podcast. Now, we still have some of the radio shows like Rick Steeves and Pauline Frommer and those sorts It's a much less crowded space, for instance, than, say, the entrepreneurial space or the marketing space or some of those things.

Chris: If you think about it, there are, as far as the place to monetize, travel is not as good in some ways as trying to teach people to help their business because people will pay for things that will make money.

Seth: Right.

Chris: And they travel maybe once a year or twice a year, sort of things. Now on the other hand, don't get me wrong, there's a great perks with doing a travel podcast like within the first five months of this year, I had been to South America, had

been to Thailand, a little bit of Spain, will go on a cruise in Alaska, and will go to Morocco and I'm not paying for any of those.

Seth: It has its benefit.

Chris: Yeah, it has its benefit. Some of the differentiation stuff has nothing to do with travel, just had to do with good podcasting. The sound quality is better in Amateur Travelers than it is with MTR sometimes. We do that because my show is generally an interview show and that makes it more likely they'll promote it. A typical, 40-minute show, five minutes actually has no bearing on it. It's typical that we cut that out and we saved our audience that much time to sort of make it more valuable for them.

Then you go to find your guest. I think that also means you got work far enough ahead, for me about a month ahead. Then when you have a guest but it doesn't work, you don't have to put that one out. I did two shows, for instance, on Poland and then neither one ever turned out because they just didn't work.

I did a show with a guy who'd been with his father who was a historian to England and the conversation kind of went like this. It's like, "Then my father and I went this monastery that was in ruins. And my father told me an interesting story about that." "Oh. What was the story?" "Oh, I don't remember." "Well, was this perhaps one of the monasteries that is destroyed by Henry VIII as he converted to Protestantism?" "Well, that could be".

Seth: You're helping him out.

Chris: I cannot edit that to anything. So partly is having a clear idea of what you're trying to do. So I get pitched all the time that would be an interesting story but they're not the stories we do.

Having a clear idea of when you listen to Amateur Traveler, this is what you hear something else.

I get to define that. I get decide. Basically in some ways, Amateur Traveler is about this destination. If you pitch me a travel company, if you pitch me a person, for instance, who's a really interesting traveler, I can tell you some of the podcast that will work for you but that's not what we do. So having some consistency of when I listen to your show, I know I will get this.

Then the other thing for me is, one of the reasons I did that, is destinations are evergreen. If I tell you about Paris, yes there's going to be a new building in Paris that's been opened, but mostly that show is a little bit of useful down the line. So last year, I had 1.3 million download, well, some of that shows that I did eight years ago, nine years ago, and ten years ago even because people are still listening to shows of other destination when they say, "I'm going to go to Prague. I wonder what Chris had to say about Prague."

Seth: They will find it.

Chris: That's strategy.

Seth: What is your biggest challenge?

Chris: Monetization is always a challenge. Most podcasters will complain about not getting enough feedback, but all we have to do is say anything controversial. Yeah. I say that's probably still the biggest challenge. It was the biggest when Paul and I met at the first podcast expo and it remains a challenge today – monetization.

Chris: In my space, I don't have a product that I'm selling. I got some ideas. I'm probably getting around some 10 years later to product creation but that's what I think, I'd be doing advertising. That means you have to keep selling it.

I've learned to get a little better at it but I'm still not that good at it.

Seth: I understand. Marketing, in our definition, is how you share your love for what you do with the world.

Chris: But you also have to have something that you're willing to charge for, right?

Seth: Correct.

Chris: The show being free, there has to be something if you pay me this money, I'll give you some value. That's why I got some ideas for product creation finally, I'd say, after 10 years.

Seth: Better late than never. The destinations may be ever green. A whole lot of your world does change in terms of travel and where people want to go, when they want to go there, sometimes, what they want to do when they get there. How do you stay on top of all of the constant few change of trends going on in the industry?

Chris: Actually, some of that changes and some of that doesn't. For instance, Las Vegas is completely re-invented since we did the first show on Las Vegas. You just have to go back to because they have changed. In terms of how you travel, the biggest changes that we've seen have been international related things in terms of you book travel and such, but since we're mostly talking about where you're going to go...

Seth: It doesn't affect you as much.

Chris: It's not quite as affected. *This Week in Travel*, which is the other show that I do is much more topical. It's more about the news this week, so it doesn't have nearly the length in terms of people listening to all that themselves unless they're interested in particular guest, so we don't get that on that show.

Seth: Right.

Chris: Because that show is topical. So a lot of people love that show, but on the other hand, it doesn't get as many downloads. There's a mix there in terms of how fresh you keep that content.

As I think about products about teaching people how to travel, then that has to be constantly refreshed with where you book travel, for instance, has changed when I would recommend just in the last year, Orbitz and Travelocity both sold. Those had both gone away, where 10 years, they were two of the big four booking entities. You never would have talked 10 years ago about *Airbnb*, those sort of things. So those things definitely change all the time.

Seth: What are the three best books you've ever read that have had the biggest impact on your work. You can't quote the Bible, which could be considered, to some extent as a travel book, and you can't put something you wrote yourselves?

Seth: Whether to travel, or podcast or marketing, any of the three.

Chris: In terms of books that I would recommend, interesting book on travel is *Lunatic Express,* the book by a guy who read the paper and so all of these obscure series thinking here and trying to here and there in third world country going up close and decided that wanted to go around the world traveling on all of those kinds of transportation the way the rest of the world really travels.

First part of the book, I don't think it's that interesting but then he sort of slows down starts getting involved with people and talks to the people in the Mumbai train in something like 10 people die a day. He talked to the guys who picked the bodies right off there and about what life is like in Mumbai and things like that. So, interesting book, *Lunatic Express.*

I think by Bill Bryson, I enjoy probably, *In a Sunburned Country*, is one of the most interesting one piece then which is all about Australia and from a very humorous point of view. Most of them, I cannot stand at my brain right now.

Seth: Okay. Well, I've done a couple pages of notes, and I'm sure our listeners have too. I greatly appreciate you being on the show. For folks who want to learn more about what you're doing, do you want them to go to iTunes and subscribe to the podcast? Is there a website that you want us to run into?

Chris: Of course. iTunes, subscribe them or go to amateurtraveler.com and we'll direct you on everything else.

Seth: Okay. Thanks so much.

INTERVIEW WITH
ADAM KRUSE

Seth: Today I have the good fortune of interviewing Adam Kruse. Adam, welcome to the show. Thanks so much for being here.

Adam: Thank you. Thank you for having me. I'm excited to talk with you today.

Seth: Can you tell us a little bit about who you are and what you're doing.

Adam: My name is Adam Kruse. I live in St. Louis, Missouri. I own a few businesses, primarily a real estate brokerage called Hermann London and a property management company and I just tried to see what kind of interesting things I can do with my time to keep me interested.

Seth: And how did you get started in podcasting?

Adam: Well, I started my podcast I guess about four or five months ago. I wanted a way for me to share a lot of the information that I have with people quickly. I wanted some way to kind of a reason to talk to some of these interesting people I see around town and kind of interview. Interviewing people or just asking questions is how I've learned so much in my career to kind of give me information that I've needed to get going, and it was kind of right place at the right time thing. I found a guy who works at a radio station and he was willing to be my producer part-time. So I'm actually going to be recording my next podcast here in about half an hour.

Seth: How have you grown your listener base?

Adam: Well, what we've done is we've – I think it's kind of one of – our efforts has been sort of a throw it against the wall and see what sticks type of thing, right. Right?

So we put our podcast on YouTube. My producer, Joey, could list out all the different places. I guess there's like a lot of different websites that he posts the podcast on and then a few that I interview actually share it with their social media connections and their sphere of influences. And so, we get extra exposure through them as well.

Seth: Absolutely. That makes total sense, all great strategies for folks to use. What do you wish you knew when you started, that you know now?

Adam: That's a good question. I suppose I wish I knew maybe how easy it would be. It's just as easy as I wanted it to be. I wonder if when I started, if we should have done the video because it wouldn't be that much harder to make our podcast have a video. I wished for one there on YouTube and one in our blog and that type of thing and I think that would help kind of get me sort of the brand recognition I'm looking for. I'm a realtor primarily and so for us our faces, our logo and our name is our brand. Maybe I wish I would have known how easy it would have been to add video, too.

Seth: I know a lot of our listeners learn more from our failure. What is then you biggest mistake and what have you learned from it?

Adam: That's a good question. I think, honestly it's been pretty easy so far, Seth. One of the only real frustrating times I think I had was when I had a guest on who I was interviewing and everything he would say, he would then like second guess and he would want us to stop the podcast and say, "Can we rerecord that? I don't know if they want to hear that. He was a real estate investor and he kept second-guessing like how the public is going to perceive what he was saying. So, I think that was probably my biggest challenge to date. I still have a lot to learn though. I think I'm in this stage what I call I don't know what I don't know. So I've got a lot to learn, and pretty soon I'll know what I don't know and I'll see how much I've got to do.

Adam: So, at this point I'm excited because once we record the podcast my producer actually types up the entire podcast. I like that, because I have extra text content on our website. If it just going to add benefit, that's fine. If it ends up and we get thousands of listeners and it will give us the business from it, I get to meet some really cool and interesting influential people, I'll be even happier.

Seth: You're not a "traditional podcaster" who might be let's say an author or a speaker in that you have a bricks and mortar physical business with physical customers that you interact for a significant amount of time to help them. Who are the types of guests you're interviewing?

Adam: Well we're mixing it up. So I've interviewed some people who are real estate investors and I tried to make those types of podcast fairly technical where we get into the numbers. I really want someone who's listening to that to actually learn something. And then we've interviewed some realtors because I think we have other realtors that are listening and I want them to hear what's working for these realtors, what's not working. How can they overcome some of these challenges without having to go through the struggle?

Then my favorite guest is this guy, Trey Malicoat who is like a strategic growth consultant. He helps a lot of our agents because we get into talking about how people work and why do these people do these things they do and what's holding us back from reaching our true potential and that kind of stuff. We try to mix it up. Today I'm going to be interviewing an editor of a local homes magazine that post about architecture and kind of local culture stuff.

Seth: Hypothetically, someone listening could say, "hey, you're a realtor. You're interviewing other realtors." Aren't they your competition? What is your mindset in your sharing what's working? What is your mindset around that?

Adam: I do think about that I was interviewing a Coldwell Banker agent on one of my last podcasts and she's talking about how great her company is. Now I understand there's friendly competition and that we can all learn from each other. But I also think there's sort of enough business for everyone. So, I'm not really worried about all of my listeners just rushing over and using her as their realtor because I think they'll be listening to all of my podcasts. Something would might go to her but they might have either way. She's doing a little bit of promoting of us because she's putting the podcast on her website and social media stuff, too. I think it's a win-win. I don't have a monopoly over real estate here and it's okay to share and honestly, maybe one day she will want to change brokers and she might consider me because of the experience she had with our podcast.

Seth: That is a mindset that I would want to have. I would agree with you 100 percent. I think you're absolutely right. I think there is enough business obviously out there for everybody and a rising tide lifts all boats. So I love that you're on the same wavelength. I agree 100 percent. Obviously, being a physical realtor in a specific market, there are trends that are affecting you, changes in your marketplace, a new shopping mall gets built or school district lines get changed. How do you stand on top of all that stuff?

Adam: Well, I guess you could say it's a little bit of a struggle.

Adam: The thing that I believe I've mastered is if I'm showing someone property in an area that is not my backyard basically, I will be an expert in finding out whatever information I need. So I know how to use the tools that realtors have available to them and know how to leverage some relationships that I made over the years to find out the information that I need to give my client a great experience and make sure they make the right kind of purchase.

Seth: What did you read every month, because I know you're always learning and always trying to grow? Are there trade journals, periodicals, magazines, newsletters that you subscribe to that sort of keep you up to date?

Adam: That's a great question. That's actually one of the questions I ask the people I interview, too. I don't necessarily have one particular news source. Go to Yahoo real estate news or something like that. I sort of utilize I guess just the emails that I get and then all of the different things that I follow on Facebook and on Twitter to see the type of articles they're posting and if I see something interesting I'll read it. So if there's an event going on around town, you're most likely going to see me there. If there's a meeting to talk about the trends in the industry, you're most likely going to see me there every day I basically show up and I'm open-minded to be hearing what's going on and so I learn a lot through that kind of thing.

Seth: What are the three best books you've ever read that have had the most impact on your work and you can't quote the Bible?

Adam: Oh, I love that. That's a good question and luckily for me, I'm sitting here right next to my library of books. I would tell you that probably if I could say every book that John Maxwell has ever written would be extremely beneficial. Visionary Business: An Entrepreneur's Guide to Success by a Marc Allen. This one had a lot of impact on me and then there's a lot, but the next one, I think you should read probably after you've had your own business for a little while, is The E-Myth.

Adam: It was amazing and I can't believe the impact it had on me and how I still tried to utilize what I learned in that book to play out how I try to grow my business and how I try to organize my business.

Seth: Alright, and those are great recommendations. The Maxwell book is now on my list. So I will go get that. I appreciate that. And for our listeners who are intrigued, rather what you're doing, first of all, I guess I should have asked where are you physically a realtor? Where are you located, geographically.

Adam: St. Louis, Missouri.

Seth: That's right. You said you're in St. Louis, Missouri and what is the name of your podcast?

Adam: The podcast we just call, we call it the St. Louis Realtor Podcast and then my company is called Hermann London, so hermannlondon.com but we operate out at St. Louis. We just recently expanded and opened an office in southern Illinois which I'm excited about. And so, yeah, I mean anyone who wants to reach out to me, it would be great.

16

INTERVIEW WITH
ANDREA CORELLI

Seth: I know you had quite an interesting journey. How did you get started?

Andrea: It all began back in the days when I was a kid. I loved music and I loved to dance. And so I tried to start as a DJ. The next step was going to work at local radio. And then I joined the music business, moved Milano. And I went to work for Universal first and then to Warner's.

Seth: Okay. So you went to work for Universal. You went to work for Warner's. What were you doing for them?

Andrea: For Universal, I was taking care of promoting and marketing all the dance repertoire. And at Warner, I was hired for a slightly more difficult project because I was going to start from scratch and develop the dance division. And so I had to take care of basically everything because there was no dance division at all at Warner's initially. So from picking the products to putting together strategies for the marketing, promoting the products and putting a whole division together. That's what I did later on, in 2005, I eventually left Warner to build my own company which I'm still working at. And the company is basically about creating marketing and promotion strategies for artists and acts in the music business with a particular focus on the dance repertoire.

Seth: How did you get started podcasting?

Andrea: My podcast is more of a passion. But one of our services is producing and distributing podcasts for many of our clients. So we teach them how to do it, what to put together, how to create content and how to distribute it, upload it on iTunes. And we even distribute them to a network of FM and web radios.

Seth: So how have you become an expert in podcasting? And how did you grow that business?

Andrea: 50 percent is being a tech enthusiast from the beginning. I joined the internet when I was at the university and it was 1993. And I have always got a close eye on what is going on in the web and the new technologies. And my daily food is TechCrunch and sites like that where I pick up all the new ideas. This combined with my radio and DJ experience made it look easy to put together something that was exactly how it was supposed to be a good radio show but transferring it to the internet audience.

And if I may add something more, the marketing side had been developing this podcast rather than the technical part. So I am able to provide to my clients a full know-how on how to build a podcast, put it together correctly, host it, upload it and then market the podcast itself because even though, especially for my clients, the podcast is itself a marketing asset, it still needs work. And you probably know that more than me.

Seth: How do you help your clients find guests for their podcast? I know a lot of podcasters are always wondering about best ways to find interesting guests to be on their shows.

Andrea: Indeed. Well, exactly, that is a part of our service. And well, to be honest, in my niche which is the music business, it is not that hard to select the right person for joining the podcast as a guest because it's quite a close circle. So you just have to find the right artist that is kind of in line with what you are doing. On the other hand, since we're always talking about big names because it has to be relevant to be useful to the podcast, it is a bit tough to get a hold of these people. But other than that, the only real suggestion that counts is make it relevant. Make it worthwhile to the listeners. If you invite someone that has got nothing to say to your audience, that's going to be useless.

Seth: How are you helping your clients monetize their podcast?

Andrea: Well, in my particular market, most of them are DJs. Some are also producers and artists. For them, the podcast is one of their promotional tools. So the more people listening to their podcast, the more clubs and festivals hire them for gigs. So it's a matter of putting together the right podcast but above everything, it is a matter of marketing you to engage more and more audiences. And this is done via many ways. The main way of course is social networks. And the second way is advertising. So my clients spend money on me for teaching them how to do the work and spend a lot of money on marketing and advertising online.

Seth: What do you wish you knew when you started that you know now?

Andrea: That's a pretty tough question. Well, I learned the lesson the hard way, I guess. And the lesson yes, its important what you do and you do it well but the most important thing is how you sell it. And this can be really adapted to any case of any job because if you're the greatest research and development technician but you can't sell what you're doing to your boss, you're going to get stuck at your level and never go up. And this works exactly the same way as any marketing. If you're the best musician in the world or if you're the best marketer in the world but the people don't get to hear what you do, you will never take a step further.

Seth: Absolutely. I think that is one of the most important lessons to learn. Since we're on this topic, what has been your biggest mistake? And what did you learn from it?

Andrea: Well, my biggest mistake I think was to underestimate my boss while I was at Warner because he wasn't really an expert in anything technically speaking. And so I was very disappointed at him because he couldn't teach me anything. All I knew, I knew it by myself. On the other hand, years later, I understood what he knew really well and what he could teach me is how to sell because he was a pure salesman. And this is what I didn't really learn from him but I had to learn it the hard way. And this is a real pity because especially speaking of business mechanics and inside the companies, it is really crucial to have the political view all the time, to know who you should stick with, to know who you shall tell what you're doing to and who to stay away from.

Seth: What's your biggest challenge now?

Andrea: Well, right now, we're working on a new social media platform which is a web application that would actually find followers for Twitter, Instagram and SoundCloud 100 percent in target with your audience and bring them to your attention. Then of course, it's up to them to decide if they want to follow you or not. But the crazy thing, the retention is absolutely incredible, unbelievable compared to what we are used to now. As you might know, for instance, a good retention on email marketing is around three percent. Correct me if I'm wrong. And with this application, you can get around 50 percent of engagement and retention.

Seth: Wow.

Andrea: It is crazy.

Seth: Sign me up.

Andrea: It is crazy and it is real because we've been beta testing over the past six months with my new clients which means that when we go bring in big clients, it's going to be even more relevant and probably their retention is going to be higher. But everybody is getting crazy about this. I've seen the light at the end of the tunnel because it's been some crazy seven months in the past for testing and putting everything together but it's probably going to be ready by the end of the month. And this is definitely my biggest challenge not at this time but ever because with – I mean it's going to be global. So I'll have to structure to put together a real heavy marketing campaign for this.

Seth: That's incredible. Sign me up as a client for that. I mean we obviously would love to use it. And I'm sure we can get a whole bunch of our clients who would love to sign up as well.

Andrea: You're invited for beta testing. You're invited as a beta tester as soon as it's ready. I promise. I'm going to give you a f ree month.

Seth: I'll happily pay for it. I greatly appreciate it. I know that trends are constantly changing for what you're doing. There's something always going on. Something's always new. How do you stay on top of everything? How do you stay on the cutting edge?

Andrea: Well, this is a tough question actually because there is no real secret about this. It's just about getting the feel and the vibe of the bits and pieces that you get from your competitors, your partners and the net. If you hear the same name three times in a week, that's for me a signal which means you have to keep an eye on that name be it a brand or personal or a network or a new technology or whatever it is. But yes, my daily fresh bread is really putting my nose in all of these tech blogs. And lately, I've been using, I love Flipboard and following the key people I have the most respect for. They always pin the right articles which I can get great information from.

Seth: I love Flipboard, a very helpful app.

Seth: What are three of the best books you've ever read and have had the most impact on your work? And you're not allowed to quote the Bible.

Andrea: Well, number 1, the *Digital Marketing Bible* which is a free eBook which you can get from HubSpot. .

Andrea: They have a ton of free eBooks with tips and practical ways to change the way you do your work and improve it significantly. And that is right now the bible for digital marketing and it's free. It's like 80 pages. You can read it in one night and it's going to be awesome.

At number 2, I'd actually put something that made me make the next step forward for what I'm doing because of combining the real technical skills together with marketing skills which is the *PHP User Manual*. I know it may sound unusual but the *PHP User Manual* together with the *MySQL User Manual* can really open a window to you. And regardless if you're going to do any coding at all on the web, it's going to save you a hell of headaches because the next time you're going to hire a programmer to do something, he could not be able to trick you. You have the PHP all the time. And I really can't say what's the third one. Maybe it's yet to be written.

Seth: That's fair enough. With everything you've got going on, if you had to run into someone in an elevator and they ask you what made you different, what would you say?

Andrea: Well, I would say that it was luck to be honest because it's really the luck of the combination of my different competencies. Pardon me if I sound a bit arrogant but I know in the music industry there is nobody that has got my technical competencies combined to the musical skills. So I can say that I have always the picture clear artistically wise and I can apply my tech competencies to that. And this is basically the difference. This is basically what makes me really unique.

Seth: That's incredible. For our listeners who want to get more from you and who want to learn more about how you're helping folks with podcast which you want them to listen to you, what website would you want them to go to? And for the folks who are interested in that new platform you're building again, where do they go to get all of this amazing information?

Andrea: Well, I think since I'm doing a lot of stuff at the same time all the time I guess the best way to reach out to me is check my LinkedIn page. On LinkedIn, I'm always open to new contacts because I know they're on there and it's business stuff. And on LinkedIn, you can always see and have the picture clear on what is going on with me because all of my projects are posted there on a regular basis. And you can contact me over there and see what I posted lately and the eBooks I read and the podcasts and everything.

Seth: Okay. Well, it's been a fascinating interview.

INTERVIEW WITH
LUIS CONGDON

Seth: Today I have the good fortune to be joined by Luis Congdon. Luis, welcome to the show.

Luis: I'm excited to be here.

Seth: Thanks so much. It's an honor and a privilege to have you here. Let's dive right in. For our listeners who don't already know who you are, how did you get started?

Luis: So I got started podcasting about two years ago, recently got really serious about it and have been loving it. It's just a fantastic way to advertise yourself and get to meet really awesome people like you, Seth.

Seth: Well, thank you for the shameless plug. I appreciate that. How have you grown your listener base?

Luis: Well, one of the best ways to grow your audience is find people who already have an audience. So when I first started,

I reached out to the biggest names I could imagine in my particular niche which is relationships. I've also branched out and started doing a podcast around business and have gotten a whole dose of movie stars, big time marketers. By doing that, you can grow your audience and really have a lot of leads generated through that.

Seth: Absolutely. Find someone who's got an audience and promote them on your show and of course they'll obviously tell their folks that they were on it. It's a great marketing strategy. I've written that one down. I know one of the things that a lot of podcasters worry about in the beginning is how do you select and find your guests?

Luis: That's a really great question and it's incredibly easy to answer. One of the best ways that I found to do that is well, first, whatever field you're in, you probably already know it pretty well. Also, if I was looking for marketers I would just, off the top of my head, I have a few names and I would Google them and find their Facebook page, Twitter page, and website page and I would write them through all the different mediums. When somebody is a pretty big name, one of the things that I've learned works really well is I go into Twitter and Facebook, I friend-request them or follow their fanpage and I start becoming an active participant in those mediums. So instead of just approaching you, Seth, I wouldn't just write you and say, "Hey, come on my podcast." Instead I would start commenting and being an active participant in your life through social media. Then when I write you, I might say, "Hey, Seth, I've been following your stuff for the last month. I really enjoyed this article that you wrote. I have a podcast and I'd love to get you on it to talk further about that article as well as the incredible work that you're doing."

Seth: That is a great way to reach out to someone. Now, I'll ask what I call the dirty question that should be the first question but then a lot of people have hang-ups about and don't want to talk about, how do you monetize your podcast?

Luis: Monetizing is a little bit more difficult than people really think it is. There's something podcasters out there like Tim Ferris, Seth Godin, Chris Ducker and some of these other people who are monetizing their podcasts. My suggestion to anybody who's really interested in doing that is first see what your fans are doing. So instead of monetizing it, see if you can get your fans to come to your webpage and follow your directions. I wanted my podcast to be a lead generator for me.

So if you come on my show or if when the movie stars come on my show, I'm not going to send my audience to another website. I'm going to send them to mine. So I'm going to say, "Hey, if you're struggling at marketing, today we're bringing on Seth." And I also want to let you know that over at my website at blankandblankblank.com we've created nifty little a cheat sheet for you. Come and check it out. You don't have to opt-in and if you like it, please opt-in and let me know what you think. I think that's a better strategy. You can also look at affiliate links, but again, I really think that you should test your market and see if they are interested in you because why else are you doing a podcast.

Seth: Absolutely. Very well said. What you wish you knew when you started that you know now?

Luis: The biggest thing that I really wish I knew was the editing process. When I first started, I didn't use a microphone. I didn't use a headset. I spoke into my computer and its microphone. I got some decent recordings from it. I used Ecamm Recorder and now I've really it stepped up and I use

Adobe Edition. I record calls directly into that through Skype and that has improved sound quality a lot. I would also say that I really wished that I knew that I could do a few plugs throughout the show.

So if I'm interviewing you for example, Seth, let's say, "Those are some great points, Seth and I want to let everybody know who's listening that because of this conversation I've created a cheat sheet or I've created an awesome video for you and you could check it out at my website," and then I would go back into the conversation. "So, Seth, let's continue hearing from you about you were saying," but don't be afraid to plug yourself a little bit because the audience is listening for you and they're excited about what you're doing and they're excited about your guest. But hopefully as they listen to your show, they become interested in you as well.

Seth: That's great advice. I clearly admit I haven't been doing that enough. I greatly appreciate that.

Luis: Of course.

Seth: What is your biggest mistake and what did you learn from it?

Luis: My biggest mistake has been around not launching. I started podcasting two years ago but I didn't actually release my podcast until about three or four months ago. So I have about 20, 30 recordings that I've been sitting on. One of the most challenging parts about that is when I do the interview with somebody, one of the things that I try to do is find a way to launch that podcast around something special. Whether it's a holiday, an event or something special to my guest. So if you came on the show, one of the things I might say is before the show I'd say, "hey, Seth, I want to let you know that these are some of the dates that I have lined up for release, but I want to ask you if you want it release at any particular time."

Sometimes my guest will say, "you know what, I'm launching a product on June 17. Do you think you could get it to me somewhere around then?" I have found that if I can release an episode based on what my guest asks, they're going to promote it a lot harder and it's a win-win situation.

Seth: I think that's a great idea.

Luis: It took me a while to learn that one.

Seth: I know you're very successful, very busy and got probably more balls in the air than you could count on your fingers and toes. What is your biggest challenge right now?

Luis: My biggest challenge has been really around increasing my output. So I've kind of gotten to a place where there's not a whole lot more that I can do without maybe hiring some extra people or trying to figure out how to automate some of my processes. So right now I'm getting to a place where as soon as I do a recording with someone, I try to edit it right as soon as we hang up and get it ready for delivery because I really want to try to minimize the amount the time that I'm spending podcasting and increasing my time with clients and other types of services that I have.

Seth: I know that you are a voracious learner, trying to keep up with the giant flow of information that comes to you every day and the constant change that it seems like everyone is dealing with on a daily basis. How do you stay on top of it all? How do you stay on the cutting edge?

Luis: I have gotten to a place where I used to subscribe to everybody's emails and try to hop on as many webinars as I could, and after doing that for a certain amount of time, I've really come to a place where I've really only want information from a few select people. So Digital Marketer for example, I like their information. They come into my inbox. I check it out when

I have time. But there's just a whole bunch of people offering you kind of the same information but it's a washed-down version. So I just try to find the people that really resonate for me and are on the cutting edge and I only take in their information now.

Seth: Great advice to help maintain your sanity, keep relevant what you're looking at and not get consumed by the clutter. What are the three best books you've ever read that have had the most impact on your work and you're not allowed to quote the Bible or a book you wrote yourself?

Luis: Conscious Loving is my favorite book on relationships. For me having a partnership is incredibly important in being successful in that area of life, and is fundamental for success in other areas of my life. *Think and Grow Rich* by Napoleon Hill is one of the most influential books for me. It's all about mind-setting. You don't have a complete life if you don't have a solid relationship and your money working for you in a way that works for you. Those are the two of my favorite books that I'll recommend to anybody who's listening.

Seth: What would you say differentiates you or helps you stand out from everyone else who claims to do some of what you do?

Luis: Sure. I think what helps me standout in the relationship field, part of it is that I'm younger than a lot of the people. So I'm just in my early 30's, so I'm able to connect with some of the people that have been around and are really research-heavy and have Ph. D.'s and doctorates and have a lot of weight in that area. They're well-known. I'm able to connect with them because I do have an education. I am a little bit older but I'm also not too old, so I also connect with the younger audience. They seem also interested in kind of what's happening in social media and what's hip right now and I think that to some degree, resonates a lot with my audience. Also, I think what resonates for people is just me, my own personality and what I bring to it that no one else can. This is Luis and you're not going to get Luis anywhere else.

Seth: That's a great answer. This has been an absolutely fascinating interview. I know how busy you are. I don't want to pick up too much more of your time. For our listeners who want to get more from you, who are resonating with what you're saying, where should we send them? What website do you want them to go to? What podcast do you want them to subscribe to? How could they get in touch with you?

Luis: Definitely. Well, I tried to brand my podcast and my websites the same, so lastingloveconnection.com and Lasting Love Connection Podcast if you're looking to get that edge on your relationship and really improve that on that. It's in the website and podcast are My Rapid Launch, and that is really helping people create online systems for their business.

Seth: Perfect. We will send them there. Thank you so much for being a part of the show. We greatly appreciate it.

Check out the Podcast Mastermind on the Next Page...

PODCAST MASTERMIND WITH
GARY OCCHINO

Seth: I'm sitting here with Gary Occhino. Which website of the many do you want to list?

Gary: It's called garyocchinogolf.com.

Seth: GaryOcchinoGolf.com. Gary, if you could just talk a little bit about your experiences with that. So far, how's it going? What's working? What have you learned?

Gary: It's been a fantastic process. When it started, I turned everything over to Seth and his team took care of everything for me. And upon the first submission of my query, people started following it. It was cool. I think it was six the first time and I liked all of them. And so I did some interviews and they've been going fantastically well. I do a podcast that involves golf and business together. So my target is to work with top CEOs. It's called the

Outdoor Boardroom: Top CEOs Tell Their Golf Life and Success Stories.

And it's just been a great conversation and it's allowed me to increase my confidence a lot in talking to these top level CEOs. It's also allowed me to be offered things I never expected would come. It's second nature to take an interest in the folks' businesses, and promoting them, and maybe asking the right questions, and showing it's really about them first. They come back and offered me certain things. One of them had offered me to play golf at her club in New York City but also to meet some LPGA pros that she's befriended.

Another one offered me to be involved with charity events which I will follow up with as far as possibly being a coach or being involved there. Another gentleman, I do some traveling with students where I take them places. He belongs to some premier clubs. He asked me if I'd like to possibly link up there. So it's been really great and I've enjoyed it and it's been fun.

Seth: I appreciate that. I'm glad that we're getting you such great results. Can you talk a little bit about how you've maybe come out of your comfort zone a little bit with working on some of the questions that you ask that we gave you?

Gary: So what's happened for me is I've been so concerned with them in the podcast that I have not asked as much about, "what's your biggest challenge in your golf game?" I'm trying to find their pain points. I'm trying to find out how I can be helpful to them and then maybe after the interview talking to them. So that was huge for me. Then just learning to be more confident in doing that, learning that there's nothing wrong with asking. I have a talented ability to help others.

So my confidence is increasing in knowing I can do that at a high level.

Gary: I've been overwhelmed by the positive response of everybody I've interviewed and how they've offered to help and "hey, what can I do for you?" And I think you saying "hey, what's the biggest challenge in your golf game and what's the biggest challenge in your business?" both of those open up – they'll talk, they'll answer. "You said earlier that your biggest challenge was your vicious slice. Would it be okay if I send you a complimentary copy of my DVD that will help you with that?" "Oh, that would be great. Thank you so much." Then they look at it and say this is great. We should really have you do X. And it will just lead to more. So I'd really like to affirm what you're doing. I think you're going to get even better results in the future.

Gary: It's a very organic way for things to evolve. It's very natural. It's not so much of trying to connect and force it. And I think people appreciate that because they know you on a personal and professional level. And they trust you. It's good. Thank you.

PODCAST MASTERMIND WITH
MICHAEL LICATA

Seth: Can you tell us a little bit about who you are and what you're doing?

Michael: Sure. My name is Michael Licata. I'm the Director of Business Development for Montante Solar as well as Montante Development, both commercial solar project developer and real estate development companies.

Seth: So talk a little bit about who your ideal client is for the solar?

Michael: We focus on commercial users who are attempting to stabilize their electric consumption or reduce the cost of their energy. It's as simple as that. A number of folks have sustainability mandates when they work for very large companies who say we have to reduce our carbon footprint by this specific amount by this period of time. And so there's an incredibly good way right now with the tax breaks, with the state incentives and the cost of power.

Seth: So your target market isn't necessarily the restaurant with one roof. You want the large institutions, hospitals, colleges, much larger and taller volume square footage of panels needed if that's an accurate term.

Michael: That would be correct. Larger installation but if they were a chain of restaurants, then it would be worth it because you'd make it up in volume. We could work with those spaces as well.

Seth: Okay. So, your podcast could be about – so it could be about reducing your carbon footprint.

Michael: It could be.

Seth: So who's the decision maker? I'm sure at some large institutions there's a committee. But who's your way in?

Michael: There are two folks who are essentially going to make the decision, the president of the company or the CFO. Everybody says they want to go green. They want to be sustainable. They want to be responsible until they see the price tag. Not unless there is a four- or five-year payback on your investment, typically, companies won't do it. So the real green that people want to go is the normal green. They want money, more money. They want return on invested capital. So the way we structure these programs and these opportunities, we get them to that return very, very quickly.

Seth: Okay. So hypothetically – we're talking about the CEO of an X size company, whatever size that is.

Michael: President and/or CFO.

Seth: Right. Well, the CEO and the CFO would have two different mindsets.

Michael: Absolutely.

Seth: And your podcast would be almost about two different things.

Michael: Sure.

Seth: So let's hypothetically pick the CEO for now if that's okay.

Michael: Go ahead.

Seth: Okay. So what would be some of his pain points?

Michael: The CEO. I'm going to back track and say CFO.

Seth: Okay. We're doing CFO now.

Michael: Let's do the CFO.

Seth: That's fine. So what are a CFO's pain points?

Michael: A CFO tends to be a linear cost oriented to reduce expenses and increase revenues. They are specific to those goals and they should be because that they are the chief financial officer and they're looking to reduce the expenses as much as much as possible and increase the revenues as much. But honestly, from the CFO's side of things, it's usually expense reduction. So the CFO is my favorite person to talk to.

Seth: Okay. So then your podcast, you'd be interviewing CFOs of successful right size companies. And maybe it's a book about the secrets of successful CFOs, maybe it's about the secrets of cost management.

Michael: How sustainability helps with the CFO.

Seth: How sustainability can increase your bottom line.

Michael: That's it. And the reason is, what I've seen is they'll hammer us in the presentations and the proposals on the cost and how we make sure that the revenue is returned, the return of investment. They market it as being sustainable. They don't say hey, we were fiscally responsible. It's all marketed as we are sustainable.

Seth: Okay. So to steal a saying from Bill Knoche's world, you sell the sizzle not the steak. So for the CFO, his sizzle is saving money but when he is going to resell it to shareholders or the community or whoever, the sizzle he's selling is we "were green."

Michael: Green and we save money. Whereas, to him, it's you're going to save money and you're going to go green.

Seth: Okay. So to him, it's save money first, green second.

Michael: Right.

Seth: But he's going to flip it when he presents it to everybody else.

Michael: He is going to say this is what we're doing to be corporate and responsible and to save money doing it.

Seth: Okay. So then you could be interviewing CFOs of companies of a certain size who are either already green and want to talk about it. Or you could probably get better results interviewing CFOs who are in the query and say something like "considering taking your company green but not sure about the cost?" This podcast is all about corporate responsibility, environmental responsibility and cost cutting and managing it all.

Michael: You can do both, right.

Seth: Yeah.

Michael: Yeah, that's great. That would be very good.

Seth: And then every week, you interview a different CFO. And one of the things I've learned is – it's funny. When I was asking all these podcasters, some of them I asked them offline how they manage their podcast. And there was one guy who said, "Oh, I use what, google to book guests but I do the urgent one because I never know what I'm doing it will be Monday. I need a guest for Tuesday and then I air Wednesday. I do everything last minute."

Michael: Priceless management.

Seth: And I said to myself, "I'm 21 weeks ahead." I did the entire book and all 21 interviews in a couple of weeks and I'm airing them one week at a time. So technically, I'm good for like the next five months before I need a new guest. So, you have two schools of thought or you could be somewhere in the middle. You don't have to be 21 weeks ahead. I would always try and stay at least like two weeks ahead. So if somebody's sick or if there's some problem, you don't have to scramble. You know you're okay for the next week before you have to find somebody.

Michael: Sure.

Seth: So can you see how that would get you in front of more impossible to reach CFOs that you probably can't get on a cold call or something else.

Michael: Absolutely. Without a doubt. That's great.

Seth: Awesome.

Michael: Thank you very much.

PODCAST MASTERMIND WITH
REBECCA POYNTON

Rebecca: Hi. I'm Rebecca from Fairview Connect. And what we do is video conferencing, video collaboration. My typical client enterprise-wide would be a CEO, CIO, CFO level. But the usage that helps the department is at a departmental level. So what I mean by that is for a podcast, what I would probably utilize this for would be training. How did video conferencing help your HR department?

Seth: Okay.

Rebecca: How did it help at the CEO travel level? How did it help each individual department successfully meet face to face, collaborate face to face as effectively via video versus traveling and getting together and conducting training seminars, etc?

Seth: So that brings up a great point. You can also use a podcast to showcase your successful clients. So she could do a case study every week of a company that used it and what benefit they got. They feel great because they were interviewed. They get to be in a book and be on iTunes and show off. And they love you for doing that and making them an example. And then you could also interview people who haven't done it yet, struggling with trying to pick a provider. And let's talk about how you evaluate providers and the questions that you should be asking your providers, which all of course lead back to you. They're skewed in such a way that the only reasonable answer is they should go to the interviewer.

Rebecca: And not even so much as "who's the provider?" It is "how is this tool going to help us, how do we utilize it effectively?" So to know other people that say "we have actually minimized our cost." And typically, you are going to significantly minimize your cost of doing business by utilizing video. But we've also done it effectively so that those that have attended the meeting via video have done it and gotten as much out of it as though we were at the same table. It's just as good as shaking hands. And that's what it needs to be – and that's where people need to overcome. It's not "who's offering the service?" as much as "how do I utilize the service?"

Seth: So yours could be educational

Rebecca: And everybody is going to want to know that. If I'm trying to do it with the HR department and I'm not sure how to do it, here's somebody who's done it very effectively and this is how they've utilized it.

Seth: Right. Which brings up another great point. Podcasts are a great stick strategy. You should interview your clients and have them talk about why they choose you, how they picked you, what work they did with you, what the results were. And they'll feel even more bonded to you that you put them on the show. And now of course, they're going to tell lots of people about the fact that they were on the show. And you've got a built-in referral without having to say, "Hey, who else do you know that we can help?" So a podcast works great also not only to get exposure and get people that you couldn't otherwise get to but they work great as a way to collect testimonials and they work great as a stick strategy as well.

Rebecca: Yeah. It's sort of a training library.

Seth: Yes. Exactly. Because then that can be a value added with your service. We're the only place that has a whole library of training content of successful users that you can go access on your phone anytime you want. And we don't even charge for it.

Rebecca: Thank you.

Seth: You are welcome.

21

PODCAST MASTERMIND WITH
BILL KNOCHE

Bill: I'm Bill Knoche. I do corporate trainings, sales training, individual sales training. You can find me at wesolvesalesproblems.com.

Seth: Awesome. Now go right ahead.

Bill: So because of Seth, a sweet spot for me is home improvement contractors. They make a lot of common errors that once you see them, they're very easy to fix and we can make a big difference in the results they're able to achieve. So I'm starting to interview home improvement contractors then I think about individual salespeople that really made a difference for and doing a podcast with them rather than doing it with the whole company to link with individual people because individuals can really catch on fire.

Seth: Yeah.

Bill: And when they're on fire, other people will listen to them because it's just about their personal success and the amazement they had with how fast they've been able to make changes. It's kind of like just holding a door open for them. They get a glimpse of something and all of a sudden they catch on fire.

Seth: So we've got your podcast that we're already doing. Podcast/book is what we should call it for home improvement contractors. You're going to start working on interviewing successful clients for your case studies. You've got a library of training content that could all be put online. And whether it's audio or video, we could get it up and just clean, edit it relatively easily. Who sees the home improvement contractor? So I'm thinking even higher up the ladder. But are there associations of home improvement contractors? Are there magazines?

Bill: Right, right.

Seth: Could we interview – here's another advanced strategy well "report the reporter". So interview the reporter who writes profiles or whatever for home improvement contractor magazine about what they do. And I guarantee you, they're going to say, "You know, that was really interesting. We should do an interview with you." "Nobody's ever asked to interview me before" because the reporter makes everybody else look good. They write the stories on everybody else but they never get any attention. So if you make them the source, flip the microphone and make them the source for the story and give them more exposure. I guarantee you a high percentage of them would come back and say, "we should put you in the magazine."

Bill: So that flips me around to talking, to interviewing PR people.

Seth: Yeah.

Seth: Talk a little bit more about that.

Bill: Well, PR people are – they're also – they don't get any time in front of the spotlight. They're always supporting other people. So going out and asking them about what's made them successful in their businesses – what's their biggest challenge in their business? Those questions.

Seth: Are they struggling to find guests? Are they struggling to write stories on deadlines? How do they manage all of that?

Bill: And then you give them a chance to give suggestions to even a small business guy that doesn't have a PR person.

Check out the Bonus
Marketing Thought Leader Interviews
on the Next Pages…

BONUS MARKETING INTERVIEW WITH
DAVID LINDAHL

Seth: Can you tell us a little bit about what you've been up
to? Because I know that you've been doing some really
innovative things.

David: Yeah. I have been investing in multi-family real estate for the
last 18 years. So I've been creating cash flows in emerging
markets throughout the United States. Buying in areas where
real estate is appreciating very rapidly, buying a property
that has a small problem and then adding a lot of value and
creating a lot of wealth in a pretty short period of time.

Seth: Awesome. How did you get started?

David: I was actually in a rock band from the age of 16-24. I left the
band when I was 24. I was tired of being broke. And from
there, I started a landscaping company. I come from Boston.
I did that for the first six months of the year. And then the

second six months, I did a bunch of odd jobs. And then I continued with the landscaping coming into the second year. And during that winter, a friend who was working for the bank asked me if I wanted to do work on a property that they're about to foreclose on. And I did and I realized that, "Damn, you know, I really don't know how to do the work but I could call contractors and subcontractors to do the work for me." And I also realized that the people who actually find the deals and are reselling them were making a lot more money than I was by doing the repairs on it.

So I went out and started learning as much as I could about real estate investing. I got a lot of online courses, late night courses. And before I knew it, I kind of geared towards multi-family because I saw an interview with Harry Helmsley from New York City who started with nothing, started buying and selling multi-family properties and ended up owning the Empire State Building.

Seth: Wow.

David: And the interviewer said, "Harry, what is it about multi-family that keeps you going?" And Harry said, "I always like the idea that a group of people would pool their money together and give it to me to pay off the mortgage on my property. And they'll give you money every month so I could pay off the maintenance guys so I didn't have to swing a hammer. I could pay off a management company so I didn't have to deal with tenants. And then, they'll give me so much money that at the end of the month I would have extra money, expendable income that I could use to reinvest, put into a savings account or just go and have some fun."

And after I heard that, Seth, I realized that there are large groups of people out there that were willing to give me money every month to buy buildings for me. I was hooked. I started buying small three- to six-unit properties and then I gradually started buying very large properties throughout the US.

Seth: That is absolutely incredible. Now, I think one of the things that set you apart is some of those seminars you went to and workshops you attended. Probably hundreds depending on the room, maybe thousands of people in the room. Some did absolutely nothing but you took action and have a completely different life because of it.

David: Yes, absolutely. I like to say you can have all the skills and you can have all the knowledge but if you're not taking action, nothing's happening.

Seth: Absolutely. Now, how do you find the properties that you are currently investing in?

David: Well, there are a lot of different methods. I like to cast a big net, kind of like marketing. But in reality, we're all in the marketing business so that we have our lead generates to suspects who become prospects. And it's the same thing with multi-family. We get deals from brokers. We get deals from owners. We get deals from management companies. We get deals from attorneys, from appraisers. Its just a matter letting them know what you do and then giving them a source to find you or to raise their hand.

So we get a lot of deals from direct mail. We get a lot of deals from brokers. A good broker relationship, that's a key in our business and then all the other ancillary relationships along the way. So we get into the classified ads. We also got into the internet. I like to do anywhere between five to seven different marketing channels a month in order to get the deals trickling in on a regular basis. So we do a lot with brokers though. It's a relationship type of business. So we have brokers that will give us pocket listing as soon as we establish the right relationships with them. And we do a lot with direct mail as well and we're dealing directly with sellers.

Seth: What do you wish you knew when you started that you know now?

David: I wish I was bigger faster. I did three to six units for about three and a half years before I even thought of doing a large unit. And the only reason I did is because I realized that I was going to lose my equity. My market was cycling and I was looking to kind of find another market that was taking off like the Boston market was when I first started. And I just started and tried to look for other markets. I had so much equity in my properties that in three years I had 41 properties. I had too much equity in my properties that I had to buy bigger properties. So I bought 40 and then I bought 120 and 350 units then realized "oh my gosh, it's just as easy to do these larger ones as it is the bigger ones and making a whole lot more money." So I would've gone bigger faster.

Seth: A lot of times our listeners learn – you learn more from your failures than you do from your successes. What has been your biggest mistake? And what did you learn from it?

David: My biggest mistake to date is an underground oil tank that cost me $161,000 to remove. And I realized that all I had to do was go to the fire department and pull the property card it will tell you whether or not there is an underground oil tank there. So I bought the property. It had the tank in the backyard and I didn't know about it. And it had been leaking for 50 years when they went to pull it out and the house was on the hill. Then the oil leaked right down the hills. So I had to remediate almost the entire neighborhood.

Seth: Wow.

David: It stressed me a lot.

Seth: That's one I haven't heard before.

David: It was painful.

Seth: Do you mind if I ask you how many units you are currently in your portfolio now?

David: Sure. Just over 8100.

Seth: What is your biggest challenge with 8100 units under your belt?

David: Well, it's the infrastructure. Here's the deal. The 8100 units, it's 37 different properties. At any given time, there is one or two properties that are always performing marginally. And even though you have 35 performing great, you're thinking, how do I get that to perform better? In all my deals now, I have investors in my deals. So, I wanted to give the investors a good return. So, the difficult part is isolating down and maybe a market turn before you're expected to – maybe there's just something going on with the property you just can't put your finger on. So those are the most difficult things right now, holding the portfolio together.

Seth: I know that you are a voracious learner and always looking to stay on the cutting edge. Are there any type – what type of periodicals, trade journals, newsletters, magazines – what do you read every month, what blogs? What do you do to keep on top of everything?

David: Yeah. I'm reading *Multi-family Millions*. So I'm reading Multi-family News and there's Multi-family Executive. There's Apartment House Finance. There's Commercial Property News, Commercial Real Estate Investor. All those are magazine that I read on a regular basis. I'm constantly out there talking to the brokers and finding out what's going on in the marketplace. I read the Miller Report and it gives me an indication of what's going on in the market through the nation and what cities are up and coming. I really love the Broker's Report. The brokers spend thousands of dollars on demographics. So I get on their list and they send me the demographics are free. So I go through all that.

Every state has a university that has a real estate center. So I'm always plugged in to that real estate center where I own properties because they're giving you the latest news releases on what's happening that may affect the real estate prices in the area like jobs, job growth. Who's moving in? Who's moving out? So I'm reading all that stuff to stay abreast on what's going in the market.

Seth: What are three of the best books you've ever read that had the most impact on your work? And you can't quote a book you wrote yourself which you'll talk about in a little bit and you can't quote the Bible.

David: Okay. My life really changed at age 26 when I started feeding myself good stuff. And actually, the first thing I heard is from Earl Nightingale called *Lead the Field*. And I know it's not a book but it was probably the thing that helped transformed my life. And then from there, you basically said it. What you feed your mind is what you become. So I started reading books like *Raise the Bar* and *The Magic of Thinking Big*, Anthony Robbins' book, *Awaken the Giant Within*. I continued to do that.

I had a low. I've been doing this for 18 years now and I had like a full year low. Yeah, I'd reached a lot of my goals and I just wasn't progressing anymore. I couldn't figure out why and I realized I wasn't doing what got me there. I wasn't reading all this motivational stuff and I'd stopped. It was almost as if I thought I knew it all. If you know it all, that's when you get in trouble. And I started rereading some of my older books and started getting some of the new stuff that's out there.

And I started reading a lot of mind books now. I'm really into rewiring the mind. There's a great book called *Super Brain* that Deepak Chopra and a guy from Harvard wrote. There's another one called *Unbeatable Mind* that was written by a Navy SEAL and that's a great book. And then another one called *Mind Power* by Kehoe. There are a lot of books called *Mind Power* but this was by a guy by the name Kehoe and that's really good. So I'm really focused on the way I think, like really focused on the way I think now and it's really helping.

Seth: Absolutely. Now, I know – you were gracious enough to tell me ahead of time that you are going make an incredible offer to our listener base. Fire away. We are exciting to hear.

David: Yeah. I've got a brand new free book on how to create cash flow in your life. A lot of people's problems are created because they don't have enough cash flow coming in. So not only will this book show you how to get a good flow but also how to create equity and wealth in your life as well. You can find it on the davesfreebook.com, davesfreebook.com. And any listener of yours Seth is going to get it for free. I think you know I've written five number one bestsellers. And so this is the sixth one coming out.

Seth: That is incredible. You've added a lot of value. We greatly appreciate it.

David: My pleasure, Seth. Thank you.

23

BONUS MARKETING INTERVIEW WITH
JON BENSON

Seth: I have the good fortune today of interviewing Jon Benson. I know you've got quite an amazing journey that you've been on over quite some time. I'm going to make you go back a little bit in time here and ask you how you got started?

Jon: Well, I got started quite by an accident. I was very interested in fitness and weight loss after going through quite a long time of being very sick, obese. And I started writing a book to just kind of express some thoughts and I had a blog. At that time, there was no such thing as a blog at that time. So my blog was essentially me updating html pages every day. I caught the eye of a guy named Tom Venuto, one of my articles I wrote on an old trainer named Vince Gironda. Caught his eye and we started exchanging emails back and forth. And I had no idea what internet marketers did. I was a graphic designer and I just didn't know. No clue at all.

And we run ads for advertising agencies and I thought that was advertising was so I was pretty clueless. Anyway, he kind of introduced me to his world and what he was doing up to and I said, "Well, you know, I have a book. I'm kind of curious if I could do the same thing that you've done," and I had no idea how much success he'd had. I just knew that he had some success. I flew up to New York to visit him and next thing I know we have a book deal and he is going to do half of it. He is going to do the marketing and the copywriting and I'm just going to write the book. And I was like, "Okay this is great". This is seems like a perfectly fair deal to me.

And he was saying all along that as soon as this hits, sure you're going to quit your job which I thought was absurd. I built the company over 14 years and at that time I thought it was doing much money making, you know, good money. Three days into the launch, I literally gave the company away. I literally just walked into my vice-president's office and said "it's all yours". I didn't even tried to sell it.

Seth: Wow.

Jon: I just couldn't believe it. I mean it was like five days when we had a data base of 35,000 people and we've shut down servers on Alexa. I mean we shut down servers and we were like a 1007 on Alexa and it was crazy back then. It set all sorts of records back then on Clickbank. So that's how I got started. And then from there, I figured out that sales copy was kind of the most important part of the whole element and figured out that I didn't know how to write sales copy.

So the reason why that first launch worked so well is because Tom didn't write sales copy. I have been studying with John Carlton for so long and had that whole formula down. And that led me to the second page of my career which is now I'm known as one of the top copywriters and that's primarily because of the VSL not because of I didn't study a lot of copywriting, I just kind of stumbled on the VSL formula that worked for a while and that became the VSL that people used to do.

Seth: What do you wish you knew when you started that you know now?

Jon: I wish I would have known that sales copy is the most important element of any thing. I really wish I would have that and drilled into my head. Tom, to his credit, certainly tried. The first draft of the letter that became Fit Over 40, he was, I read the letter and I was like, "First of all, I want to meet this guy. I don't know who he is." It didn't sound like me.

Seth: Right.

Jon: And second of all, like no one's going to read a six thousand word letter, right? It's the same thing everyone says, right? I wish I would have known exactly how important that was because I went into years of just trial and error, losing who knows, how many hundreds of thousands of dollars trying to write less salesy or right in a more cozy way, and it just doesn't work. It certainly doesn't work in most fields. So I wish I would have understood the gravitas of knowing having what I called words to get cash on your page, but also using those, that same persuasion power that a lot of guys can. They write those kind of words but they use it to curse rather than compel. And so, my take on it is really compelling and dynamic and core value attracting language that does I think a better job of selling that also aligns with integrity and congruity of your products.

So if I would have known that early on, and if I would have really had the ability to say, "I'm just going to focus on one thing at one time". So those are the few things you asked for what I give you to. It is very difficult for me to focus on one project at a time, I was like "let's do this, then let's do this, and let's do this." And again, Tom was saying, "Dude, I would just do this whole Fit Over 40 thing." I was barely 40-years-old when the book came out and I just think this did not feel like it was the right fit. And looking back, that would have been the most lucrative by far, I mean.

Seth: What is your biggest challenge now?

Jon: Well, the biggest business challenge now would be, for me, it's always been getting qualified traffic to the sales pages that we know that can work the best that have nothing to do with affiliates. So I always had a very lucrative affiliate model and basically blew off sales traffic or buying traffic and just never really got into it. There's some sort of mental barrier there. I was even taught everything back in the heyday by a friend of mine. And he literally said, "Here's exactly how I do it, and how exactly to set up your campaign," and it still bombed.

We know it wasn't because of the stuff he was doing because, a) it was working for him buying traffic for me. So it's like, it was really weird. So that has definitely been a challenge.

The other challenge is simply to have enough tech, enough of the people who can pull things off faster because a big part of my company is tech and software and we really have only a few guys working on that. We need more and it's on platforms that are unusual and it's either they are very pricey or they were flakey. So there was the flaky programmer thing from almost from day one. I am lucky to have the guys that I do, so the two bigger challenges.

Seth: I mean your 'accidental launch' broke all kinds of records, what has been your most successful ones since then?

Jon: Definitely the "Every other day diet" was the first video sales we have ever written. So that one freaked everyone out because it started the whole VSL thing. So I wrote that and I was playing around with the idea of putting words and text together in a certain way. Basically the idea was how can we get really low streaming quality video working? What I added I knew about persuasion, my work in NLP, etc. No one likes to read but people liked to be read too and all those things I knew were kind of prevalent and thought what if there's a way that we can make that sale.

So it was a lark. I didn't test anything, I just kind of threw it up and when it worked, it worked to such a huge degree that the book went from non-obscurity, it was like top 20 maybe but it went from like the written sales page which I tried to write to the VSL that I wrote just shot up to like number one. And it was like, within 30 days where people were spending millions of dollars on traffic for me and it was a different, you know, many zeros added to the bank account and kind of a different lifestyle.

And that was right before the infamous Google Slap. So I had about five or six months of writing that way where my friends had like years of writing that Google way and they were able to bank millions, upon millions of dollars. And right when that Google crash happened. It was so – it felt like a punch in the gut, right. Like you finally hit this huge massive homerun and then Google just pulls all the weight loss out from everybody because of the acai berry assholes and the guys that were just doing scamming kind of marketing.

So guys who were in the good side of the fence, you know, myself and Mike Geary and those kind of guys. We all got trampled along in the process and what Mike decided to do was go on and try to figure out how to make this weird little thing that we were just playing with called Facebook. Work which we all said, "No, that will never work for traffic."

So he'd open the banner ads and Facebook ads and all that and I just said, "You know what, there are so many people asking me to write these VSLs for them now and its very lucrative. I can do it very quickly. I'm going to dive into this and see if there is something here because IM makes more money than fitness.

And so, we went on two different paths and so for the last five years, I've been primarily the IM space and ended up writing some of the top letters out there in every space, in multiple spaces and I kind of got turned into a legend. I guess you could think rather quickly just because of the nature of how, you know, if you create a way of marketing that's different, people start remembering who you are. And so, that took off and now I'm kind of going full circle back to fitness and doing the Sellerator and the teaching that I do in the video sales world.

Seth: The rate of change is increasing so rapidly in our industry and you touch so many different industries and you've got to keep up on so much, how do you stay on the cutting edge?

Jon: Well, my focus used to be only how do I stay on the cutting edge and now, its like how do I find the people who are on the cutting edge that I can get to do it for me. It's a more powerful question for me and ask – as far our own tech stuff, the Sellerator stuff which is software that teaches you. It's a system inside a software. The software is secondary to the system.

The training is extraordinarily important and it's just couched inside. So it's not as important for the software side of our stuff to stay on the cutting edge. As far as the other industries and things like that goes, my whole focus is really on copywriting and fitness.

So I don't write letters for other people anymore. I just retired from that last year and I want to just focus on what we do very well which is help other people write their own letters rather than paying me several hundred thousand dollars to write letters for people. I can teach you how to do this for a lot cheaper and that's been the business model that we've used for Sellarator and then for our own stuff, you know, it's just more fun to do it.

You know, fitness and stuff and diet is really not much to stay on top of for being cutting edge. I mean, not much changes. They are still pretty much the fundamentals, right?

Seth: I know you're obviously a voracious reader and a constant and never ending lifelong learner, what are the three best books you've read that have had the most impact on your work and you can't quote a Bible or something you wrote yourself?

Jon: *The War of Art,* Steven Pressfield wrote that and that's been – that's like whenever I start getting out of the groove, I just go back to that book and read that. Along the same line is a book called I believe its called *The One Thing* could be called *Your One Big Thing.* I'm drawing a blank on the title so if you don't hold me to the title of that and *Mastery.* The book called *Mastery* by Leonard. So those were my three favorite books outside of copywriting.

So we go into the copywriting, you know, we go into things like *Scientific Advertising,* and that kind of thing. But as far as just books and journals for keeping and going, those are the three because that happens to be the three things that I also struggle with. I struggle with consistency in one thing because you're being a creative guy, you kind of get bored with it, right?

And so, the more consistent that I find myself to be the more centered I find myself to be – I always end up being more productive even if I don't like the process sometimes. So I just keep reminding myself with those three books.

Seth: I would agree with that wholeheartedly. For our folks who are listening a lot more from you, who want to enroll and learn how to write those amazingly high converting VS launch breaking records setting VSL themselves, what is the best place for them to consume more of Jon? What is the best place to get in touch with you?

Jon: Best place is still going to be sellerator.com and that is our interface site. When you go there, it looks like your typical pretty website as opposed to your hardcore direct marketing site. We put people through a funnel and it gives them – gets them to the hardcore direct marketing website but we wanted the interface side because we're getting a lot of corporate teaching now. We have like a billion dollar hotel chain who wants us to train their guys on how to sell on the phone, for example, and how to use video sales letters and send people to, you know, video sales letters on the phone. And so because of that, you kind of one of the prestige looking site but we took a kind of a fun approach to it and still give it a real hard marketing feel too. But that's the best way to reach, just find out more of what we do and the packages that we offer and how it works.

Seth: All right.

Jon: So we factor with the billion dollar threshold which we're pretty proud of - that's a billion dollars for marketers like you guys.

Seth: Well, we greatly appreciate that. Benson of Sellerator.com, thank you. It's been an honor to interview you. Thank you so much for allowing us to pick your brain and learn from you.

Jon: Seth, thank you. I appreciate it.

BONUS MARKETING INTERVIEW WITH
PERRY MARSHALL

Seth: I have the amazing good fortune today to be sitting here with one of my mentors, someone I have seen on tape, someone I have been a client of, someone whose books, products, coaching programs and membership sites I am a member of, someone whom I cannot consume enough from, the legendary Perry Marshall.

Perry: Wow, that's quite an introduction, thank you. It's great to be on here. Glad you're spreading the good word about accountable advertising and getting as much bang for your promotional buck because it matters. So it's a pleasure to be on today.

Seth: I appreciate that. I agree a hundred percent. Yes, I believe it is part of my mission to help business owners free themselves from the marketing vultures that you also fight against. For those folks among our listeners who might have been living under a rock, your star has been on the rise for quite some time. I'll make you go back with the short version to the beginning. How did you get started?

Perry: The story really begins right after my job as an engineer with a pregnant wife and ended up going into sales. I'll go into technical sales— I'm way smarter than all those sales guys. This should be easy.

Seth: Well, sir, you're an engineer.

Perry: I was in for a rude awakening, yes. And ultimately, funny thing is that all that engineering background really did eventually come in handy. In fact, really the 80/20 book is an engineering. But it took me about 15 years to figure that out and really the 80/20 Sales and Marketing book is hopefully 15 years of pain and suffering that somebody else won't have to endure. You either go into sales or marketing, or start a company of whatever variety.

There's a lot of anguish that you can spare yourself if you pay heed and eventually I discovered Direct Response Marketing. It was about two years into my sales career and I was about to get fired and I did get fired. Fortunately, I was starting to get a clue and I took a different job and they actually let me use some of the stuff I was learning. That became a really amazing success story and the rest is history. That's how I got started.

Seth: Absolutely incredible. I think the 80/20 Sales and Marketing book is on my list of top three business and marketing books of all time. I've read it at least five times and keep reading it, and every time I go through it, I learn something new. It makes me more money and gets me and our clients better results.

Perry: Well, I'm glad you say that because in the current atmosphere of Facebook and social media and everything, it's like people are just inhaling information at blinding speed. Really it's about mastering a few things and not gorging yourself with everything. And so, you're actually reading this book five times, it is the kind of book you can read five times. Not so many books like that but that's really going to pay off. I know it's probably self-serving but –

Seth: You're supposed to be self-serving. We're marketing people.

Perry: That's right but it really helps other people, like just sit down and master this book.

Seth: It's funny that you mentioned that because I have been a lifelong martial artist. I'm a black belt in Krav Maga, which is from the Israeli military and one of our sayings is a black-belt is not someone who knows 10,000 different ways to throw a punch. It's someone who's really practices one punch 10,000 times.

Perry: Well, Bruce Lee said something really similar to that, right? "I fear not the man who knows 10,000 techniques. I fear the one who has practiced one kick 10,000 times". It's seeing that there's an 80/20 hiding under almost every nook and cranny. It's everywhere. It's sitting there outside the window that you're looking through right now. It's everywhere but you need to see it for what it is and then you can start to harness it.

Seth: With all of the experiences that you've had all from your original conversion from an engineer to direct response marketer, to becoming arguably the king of Adwords, to 80/20 now (which obviously can be applied to anything) if you had to pick one thing you wish you knew when you started that you know now, what would it be?

Perry: I wish I had known myself.

Seth: That's not what I expected.

Perry: And this really applies to everybody. I believe that everybody has their own peculiar way of selling.

When I started my first sales job, I was sitting there pounding the phone, pounding the pavement and trying to get in to see people and I managed to get in to see them but I was positioned horribly. What I learned about myself – and this is very painful. It cost me a lot of money. It cost me a lot of stress. It almost made us bankrupt was that I am a consultative salesperson. I sell with knowledge and solutions. I remember one time we were going to this meeting and I was with my boss and everybody was introducing themselves and I shook a guy's hand. I said, "Hi, I'm Perry. I'm an electrical engineer," and my boss goes, "Perry's the sales guy. Sometimes he kind of forgets what his job is."

It's like a smack in the face, right? I was not a person who could just show up, tell some jokes, buy somebody a drink and ask for the order. My conscience literally would not let me do that. I need to be here solving a problem, making something better, using my brain, really serving the customer and I was not in a job that really allowed me to do it. What I really started to figure out over time was that what we sold at that company did not have a strong unique selling proposition. It wasn't something where – if you had the right amount of elbow grease and the right amount of ingenuity that could you go solve somebody's problem and be the hero. We were just selling stuff kind of like out of a catalogue, and that did not fit me. Interestingly, I had gone to this retreat that we've done at church.

Somebody at this church had put together a very sophisticated self-inventory of what's your giftedness and what should you be doing. I go on this retreat. I come home with this notebook, with all this really good stuff but I was not mature enough to recognize it. I'm like, "Well, I don't really need to do that". I stuck the notebook in my basement and I went on to try to do it Perry's way. When I was almost bankrupt and about to get fired from my sales job, I pulled out that notebook and I started to realize, you know what? I already figured out what I should be doing and how I should be, so I started to pay attention.

One of the things it said, for example, is that I'm a good writer. At that time, I had no conception that that was useful to anybody at all. When I discovered Direct Response, I discovered you can sell by writing. You could write a sales pitch. You could write a sales letter, a full-page ad or eventually an e-mail or a webpage. There was all these gifts that I had that I wasn't using and I was actually working in a place where they did not value who I was and what I did. To fast forward the long way, so now, I've consulted in more than 300 industries and I've done all these different things and I started to realize there are different kinds of marketers. There are different kinds of sales people.

Some people sell by being a hostage negotiator. You throw them in a situation and they just solve it, right? They schmooze people. They do whatever. They negotiate. Other people sit in a cave and craft the sales letter for two months. Other people make a video. Some people show you spreadsheets, numbers and proof. Other people pluck your heartstrings. You hear what I'm saying?

I had to help people figure out how they do it and eventually I created this tool called the Marketing DNA Test and it costs 37 bucks but there's a link to take it free inside the 80/20 book. When I go to an audience, I'll say, "How many took the test?" and hands go up. I ask, "How many of it – it nailed you?" and two-thirds of the hands will stay up. If I could have understood about three years faster what I really did well and how I should be selling, I would have spared myself so much agony.

I have to tell you when I go two years working at this company and barely sold anything beyond just the little things that kind of show up, never hitting any homeruns, almost never making any money above my base, I was so ashamed of myself. I was so frustrated. What is wrong with me? How come Wally and Fred and Mike sell so much stuff and I'm far behind everybody else. What is my problem? You don't have to do that. I mean there's probably a certain amount of that in life that's inevitable but it doesn't have to last for two or three years.

Seth: I would agree a hundred percent and there's quite a few writer-downers in that answer. I'd like to address one of them. You talked about the church retreat you went on and the self-analysis and self-inventory that obviously later connected and inspired the Marketing DNA. Let me ask you this. How would you compare and contrast that search retreat you went to to the work you're doing now. It's like the Sozo ministry that I went through the workshop in Chicago. It absolutely blew my mind and changed my life.

Perry: There are really two completely different things in what you just asked. So one of them is knowing yourself and understanding – there's a lot of really good tools out there.

The Marketing DNA test is one of them, but just to make it really generic, even like the Myers Briggs, the ENFJ and all that, if you sit down with the person who knows how to use that tool and you talk to them, like a certified person whatever, you can really make a lot of progress and get a lot of insight. In fact we have a person on our staff named Rebecca and she does that with people with the Marketing DNA test. And so that's one kind of thing and like that, know yourself. *You can never actually understand any customer any better than you understand yourself and that is a great truth*. You must know who you are, what you're good at, what you're not good at, what you should be doing, what you should not be doing.

Now, you mentioned Sozo. Now, that's a whole different conversation but I'm really glad you brought it up because as I started to get a little bit of success in my own career. Then I started doing consulting. Inevitably I find myself coaching and consulting with all kinds of other people. It took it a while but I started to recognize that a person could learn most of what they needed to know to be successful in marketing in about two to three years, maybe even less if they were sharp. They could learn the techniques and they could learn how to buy the clicks and they could learn how to make a webpage and get some sales pages up or whatever. But whether they were successful with that or not ended up being dependent on how clear their mind and their emotions were about being successful and whether their self-image would allow that to happen or whether their inner head trash was going to kill him.

I remember – again, this is that same sales job that I really struggled with. Probably one or two months into that job, I was still pretty new and I was still pretty excited about this job, we had a meeting in Detroit that I needed to go to and I needed to get up early and catch the plane and go to Detroit.

I wake up and it's like eight o'clock in the morning and my plane takes off in three minutes and I haven't even gotten out of bed and I'm missing my plane and I'm looking at the alarm clock and you know that feeling when the adrenaline surges through your body when you made a giant screw-up like that. Oh, my word. What am I going to do, right? I get there in an hour late and then I have to rent a car and I get to the meeting and I'm late. My boss is trying to figure out where I am and all of these. I went back and I'm like, what happened to my alarm clock?

I went back – when I got home that day, I figured out the only possible explanation was that I had punched the off-button on the alarm clock, which I would never normally –

Seth: Right. You wouldn't consciously think to do that, right?

Perry: No, I would never normally do that. In a normal day, I never did that but on that day, I did it. That was self-sabotage.

Seth: Subconscious, right?

Perry: It was subconscious rollover in your sleep. People do this, okay. They do all this work and all this stuff and then in a moment when they're not paying attention or whatever, they shoot themselves in the foot with a .44, like boom! People do this all the time and I watched people do this, and you're like, okay, so what do you do? Do you stand in front of the mirror and recite, "I'm good enough. I'm smart enough. People like me." What do you do about this?

I started making some connections because as I got into my 40's, I also started to see that I had lots of friends, including family members where stuff happened to you a long time ago and now you're acting it out in your adult life. Somebody was sexually abused. Somebody was physically abused. Somebody had an alcoholic parent and you know that whole drama of dysfunctions and things, right? I slowly started to figure out that when the guy's 45 years old and he divorces his wife and he drives Mazda Miata and he's got a 30-year-old blond girlfriend. Then that only lasts for eight months. Then he goes crashing through all these boundaries. It is life. A lot of that is like unresolved crap that he never dealt with and it's forcing him to sit up and pay attention, right? I started to realize this is the kind of stuff that really trips people up and I started to realize that stuff – somebody's midlife crisis and that head trash that made me push the off-button on my alarm, it's the same thing.

For a while, I was really discouraged. It's like, "Wow". You know, I got all these friends and when I actually get to know them well enough to know what's really going on in their life, almost everybody I know has this crap that they don't know how to get rid of. It was really depressing.

Some of that same crap came pretty close to costing me my marriage. I got to get really serious about this and find out – and I went on this like wild search for solutions and when you're in that kind of pain, you go looking around and there are all these things out there. There's tapping and there's NLP and there's hypnosis and there's psychotherapy and the list goes really long. You could get on drugs, right. All these things you can do and the most effective thing that I ever found was this really interesting and in fact remarkable simple model that's done by prayer counselors called Sozo. I saw people who – they had stuff they could not get rid of – addictions, phobias, and this stuff would go away.

Sometimes overnight, not usually, not necessarily but it was exponentially more powerful than anything else. I said to myself – first of all, I started getting into it, but secondly, it's like, you know what – if this could heal somebody who was molested by their brother when she was 8 years old, then this can solve people's financial head trash.

Seth: Right, right, small by comparison.

Perry: That's what happened and if you go to perrymarshall.com/headtrash, I have a whole e-mail series where I start to peel the onion on that. I believe that people sabotage themselves because their identity is messed up at a spiritual level and they don't know who they are. Now, I've been talking a while, but you've actually kind of – you've delved into this, too. Why don't you talk about it a little? I'm sure you got your own way of describing it.

Seth: I do, not as eloquent as yours perhaps. I haven't written a copy on it but you have. However, it has significantly impacted my life in that I found limiting beliefs around financial stuff around money that I didn't know I had, some from my parents, some from other places, mother, father, sister, brother, preacher. It was amazing that you don't realize all of the crap that's in your head is holding you back and so you learn how to dig down deep enough to identify it and realize, "oh, I didn't realize that I thought that and that I was taking action, like subconsciously punching the alarm clock because of that." I'm sure you may have had a similar experience.

I have this memory, some different parts of, let's say from the age of 22 backwards, in regards to relationships, things my parents said or acted or did in regards to money. To me, some of them are some of the most difficult experiences of my life and it significantly shaped what I did for the next 20 years. There was one thing that happened I think when I was probably 13 or 14. My father said something to me and it affected how I felt about myself in that area for decades, and probably to a certain extent still does but much less. When I finally brought it up to my dad a few years ago, he was like, "Oh my God, I don't even remember that. What are you talking about? I never said that."

Perry: Right.

Seth: Well, I've been upset about it for 20 years. What do you not remember? That was traumatic. I'll give you one example. One of them is completely unrelated to money. I had taken my bar mitzvah money and bought myself an electric piano and I wanted to learn to play the piano and I was playing all of the time and singing along. I was in all the plays and musicals and at one point, my dad had come into the living room. When I started learning the piano, I went to my first piano lesson and the teacher starts with, "This is note C and this is D." I said, "No, no, no, that's not what I want. I'm a Billy Joel freak. I want to learn – my favorite song right now is We Didn't Start the Fire. I want to learn how to play that." "Well you have to start at the beginning." I said, "No, teach me everything in regard to playing this song." And she said, "Okay, fine." So, I learned to play the piano by learning to play Billy Joel and I played that song eight million times. I could play it blindfolded. I could switch hands and play with the opposite hand because I knew it so well. So I'm sure that my father, when he said what he said, said it in regards to after hearing We Didn't Start the Fire for the 87th time in a row, and was probably tired of hearing of it but he came into the living room and was like, "Turn that off. You can't sing." And to me, it I took it as my father being a music critic telling me you can't sing, and got this incredible fear over singing in public and singing at all.

My first undergraduate degree was in acting and I went to one of the top three acting schools in the country, but I majored in acting instead of musical theater because I was afraid of singing because he told me I couldn't sing. Then when it manifested itself significantly was at my wedding and I took what was – one of my wife and my favorite songs at that time was a song called I Never Saw Blue Like That Before. My wife was obsessed with the color pink. I re-wrote the lyrics to be I Never Saw Pink Like That Before and I sang it to her at our wedding and I was freakin' terrified. The whole morning doing pictures, being outside, me greeting everyone when they come in before the ceremony. I went and hid in the temple library. I didn't want to talk to anybody. My wife was freaking, going "Oh my God, does he not want to marry me? Does he have cold feet? What is the problem? Why isn't he out in his gregarious self and talking to everybody? He won't tell me what is wrong. He looks great in a tux but looks like emotionally, he looks like toast. Like what the hell?" And she didn't know at that time.

I was terrified because I was going to sing at the reception. I did it anyway. I may have had a little bit of pharmaceutical help. It's a good thing she probably doesn't listen to my podcast too much because I don't know if I ever told her that. But I sang, got through it, didn't die. The earth didn't open up and swallow me whole. Everybody applauded and it was a couple of years after that, we were talking about the wedding I think and I was like, Dad, you know the reason I was so scared was because you said that. He was like, "I don't remember saying that. What are you talking about?" It was like, holy crap. I've been carrying this around with me. Then I started doing your stuff, like the Sozo stuff, I was like, Oh my God. First of all, is he even a credible source? You're not a music critic and critics sucks anyway. He is not a Broadway star. He's got no basis for evaluation. I'm like I can feel right now like I still have a tiny bit of stuff around it but it's much less than it was to the point where – my wife is like, "Oh my God, is he going to run out of the wedding? What the hell?" And it had nothing to do with her. It had to do with unresolved crap in my head from my dad.

Perry: This just shows that how something affects you has almost no relationship whatsoever to the size of the original event.

Seth: True. I mean it was literally 10 seconds.

Seth: I would assume that if I ever had a conversation with dad about all the crap he dumped in my head about money, he would probably realized that much more, because he would hopefully realize his own issues about money and that be aware that some of them existed. I remember I got into Syracuse, SU, top three drama schools in the country but absurdly expensive. My dad was freaking out, "Oh my God, how are we going to pay for this?" And then my mother would always be the one to be, "It's okay, you can go. We know it's your dream. Go for it." Every semester it would be my dad who'd give me that panic phone call when the tuition bill came. "I don't know if you're going to be able to stay there. You might have to come home and go to UB, University of Buffalo. You might have to come home and transfer. I don't know–" and I would freak out and call my mother, "What the hell?" And she's like, "No, no, no. It's going to be all right. You're going to stay. Don't worry about it." Four years of that. So obviously that affected my belief about money because my parents had a scarcity complex.

Perry: Most of our parents did.

Seth: Right, which they learned from their parents who grew up in the depression. My mother-in-law hordes Kleenex because during the depression they didn't have any Kleenex. Her mother always horded Kleenex once they could afford it, so she hordes Kleenex and if you ask her why, she'll tell you. "Oh, it's because my mother didn't have any in the depression." But that doesn't stop her from buying 20 boxes just in case they run out. Nobody ever blows their nose that much in their house, but you never know.

Perry: Wow, well so – when I listen to that, I totally relate. I had one of those incidents about playing drums with my dad, which I won't go into. We can all sort of probably imagine but I sit there. I think what chance do any of these parents have of not inflicting some kind of damage on their kids –

Seth: Right. You've got a ton of kids. You've adopted. You have your own. My wife and I have three and I'm thinking. Am I saying anything to my 8-year-old son today that's going to wind him on the couch in 20 years or affect his future? So I'm like I know at some point there's got to be things that I will have done. I'm doing my best to be aware of my own issues and not put them on them but obviously nobody's perfect and nobody is completely free of everything. Otherwise, we'd be on a mountaintop, communing with God or something.

Perry: Well, Seth, what this just really means is that our kids need to learn how to go do their own clean-up. It's very important to point out that yes, all of us, we get damaged by people and sometimes the damage is unintentional and sometimes the damage is malicious, but ultimately we have to take responsibility for our belief systems and for cleaning out whatever we've believed that's not right.

We can't be victims. We can't lay the blame on other people. Again, sometimes it was very innocent. Sometimes the person is as guilty as all get out. But either way we got to forgive them. We've got to move on and we got to untangle whatever we believed because what I discovered about this stuff was the issue is not the incident itself. The issue is what lie did you start to believe about yourself and your identity that came from the incident, and that's the part I own. That's the part you own, right? And so you've gone out of your way, like I'm going to untangle my belief system. I'm going to get this straight and I'm going to stop doing this so that I can be more of all I was made to be.

Seth: Absolutely. You mentioned it earlier. You talked about people inhaling information and that the lies of everything we're inundated with on a daily basis. How do you, of all people, how do you stay on the cutting edge?

Perry: The funny thing is I don't pay hardly any attention to all the marketers and business gurus and everything, very little. I start my day by journaling, praying and meditating and usually for the first hour or two of the day. That's my only input. Then I'm very deliberate about, okay, I'm going to read this book.

Now, I might be in the middle of five books at a time, but I'm very deliberate about that and I'm also very 80/20, not even just daily, 90 percent of the value is going to come from probably 10 percent of what I can read.

I have a bookshelf for these are the books that I intend to read soon and I'm very selective about who I listen to. You don't need to follow these 75 different people on Twitter. You

don't need to be on 26 different e-mail lists. It's actually –
there's very few people like I can count them. The people
who can be on 30 different e-mail lists and actually pick and
choose and parse and decide between them all, I could count
on one hand. There are people that can do that.

Seth: I can say we probably know both of them.

Perry: And we, yeah – we probably know both of them, but most
people, you need to pick somebody who makes sense to
you that you can follow and you learn their lingo and
you learn their way of doing things and you make sure
it's compatible with who you are in the Marketing DNA
sense and you ignore almost everything else. You might
give it – everybody else, you might give 10 percent of your
attention to and that's the 80/20 learner. The most valuable
stuff is going to come from a very, very small number of
influences. Of all the books that you own in your library or
whatever, there's two or three of those books that are worth
reading five or ten times.

Seth: Well, you just segued into my next question. What are the
three best books you've ever read that have had the most
impact on your work and you cannot quote a book you wrote
and you cannot quote the Bible?

Perry: Okay, okay.

Seth: Those are my rules.

Perry: All right. Let me just – since I can't quote the Bible, let me just
say that one of my rules is the 300 years rule, which is I had
to spend some of my time everyday reading something that's
more than 300 years old because that's a great litmus test. It's
passed a lot of muster, right? That's kind of the problem with
our social media world, is everybody wants something that's
new and most of it is just ridiculously irrelevant.

Some really great books – one of the absolute best and the most underrated book, a business book I've ever read is *The Star Principle* by Richard Koch and Richard wrote the original 80/20 book that set my mind on fire, but his book, *The Star Principle* is really his wealth formula. He's worth 270 million dollars.

Seth: You had him speak in a recent event.

Perry: I had him in to speak in an event, which was great. Read *The Star Principle* and there's actually – we have a little quiz at starprinciple.com that you can take and you can score your business. It's like you can ignore most of what you know about business and just focus on *Star Principle* and it will really, really move you forward.

Okay. Other books that are really essential, there's not very many. Certainly one that's worth mentioning is *On Writing* by Stephen King. That's an all-around great book on writing and it doesn't matter what kind of thing you need to write. I might have to think a little longer to come up with some other business book –

Seth: That's all right. Those are just great recommendations.

Perry: Yeah.

Seth: And for our listeners who want more from Perry Marshall, who were fascinated by this conversation, where do you want them to start? Where do you want us to send them first?

Perry: Go to sell8020.com and just get a copy of 80/20 Sales and Marketing. We have a very special price there. It's less than the Amazon. It comes with some extra things that you wouldn't get if you're just buying it on Amazon and then, pay attention to how we sell to you after that. We're very strategic about building relationship with customers. In fact, you see this in our Amazon reviews for the book. People say, "I got in Perry's list and have almost then subscribed a couple of times but then every now and then, he comes up with this really insightful thing that I'll get in my e-mail." We strategically plant those things there. It's very deliberate on our part. There's nothing accidental about it.

Seth: Okay. This has been absolutely incredible and a wonderful opportunity. I greatly appreciate you being on the show. I got pages of notes. I got a ton out of it. I know our listeners did well. Thank you so much.

Our special guest has been Perry Marshall of sell8020. com. I actually have bought the book for members of my own mastermind group. I have probably worn out my own copy of it because so many pages are dark here and highlighted and have them put notation notes on them. So do yourself a favor and grab a copy of it. Thank you so much for being on the show, Perry. It's really been an honor.

Perry: Thank you very much. It's a pleasure, and great questions. I appreciate you talking so candidly about the piano and your dad and all that. I think that's going to help some people.

Seth: If it helps one, I did my job.

Perry: Excellent.

25

BONUS MARKETING INTERVIEW WITH
SALLY HOGSHEAD

Seth: Today, I have the amazing good fortune of interviewing the one, the only, the legendary Sally Hogshead. Sally, welcome.

Sally: Hey, Seth. I am excited to get going on this. Let's make sure that by the end of this podcast, the people know how they can be applying their natural advantages not only to their direct selling, their marketing but in all the different areas of their life. Are you game?

Seth: I am all in.

Sally: Okay. Bring it on.

Seth: So let's dive right in. For those of you who have been living under a rock and don't know who Sally is, she is the bestselling author of *Fascinate: Your 7 Triggers to Persuasion and Captivation* which has been translated into over 12 languages. She has two more books. One of which is about to come out, I believe. She's a world class branding expert and bestselling author. The new book is *How The World Sees You* which is a New York Times bestseller. And she is hiding in a cave right now and we interrupted her cave time where she's finishing the third book.

Sally: I came out into the sunlight from the cave to talk to you.

Seth: Yes, I greatly appreciate that. She is the creator of the Fascination Advantage Assessment, the world's first test that measures how you fascinate which has helped over half a million participants discover their natural advantages of persuasion. So I'm going to dive right in. What do you wish you knew when you started that you know now?

Sally: I wish that I had known that sometimes the greatest business opportunities are not the ones that are the goals that you initially set out to achieve. Like when I thought I wanted to release my last book *Fascinate*, I thought that I wanted to build my own business around almost like a business model of an advertising agency helping people create the right language, attract better customers, be able to charge more for their products. And just sort of as a little side experiment, I decided to do a personality assessment that would measure the communication cues that you're sending to the world that shape how people perceive you. It will be a marketing based assessment instead of a psychology assessment. And it was really an experiment, kind of a beta launch. It's just a side thing that I did as a pet project to drive social media around the book launch.

Well, what I realized though is this assessment that measures communication was not only way more profitable and way exciting but it was personally more fascinating for me to be building my business around. So I shifted my entire business in a one year period and stopped working with clients in creating their marketing messages in a customized consultative way. And instead, I helped them identify their own advantages, their teams, their brands and so on through this assessment and this system. And I couldn't have known that at the beginning. And so I wish I had known it is important to look at the side opportunities that are developing. As you're building the bridge, you may find that bridge leads you to a different place when you initially started. And it's important not to get locked in on achieving the goal for the sake of the goal.

Seth: That is absolutely true. Sometimes, the side opportunities end up being bigger businesses than the ones you started.

Sally: As entrepreneurs, it is important for us – as people in marketing, you have to always understand that when you go into any type of an endeavor that you can't know what's going to happen as the steps start to put themselves together. And I'll give you a very personal example. Last year, my daughter, Azalea, she is 11 years old. She fell down and she hit her head and she had a concussion. And for almost a year, she couldn't go to school, she couldn't work on the computer. She had to take a leave of absence and she was absolutely devastated. We talked to pediatric neurologists and craniosacral massage and there were three doctors' appointments a week. And I kept saying to her, "We just don't know where this is leading. We don't know why you fell onto your head. We don't know how this is going to turn into something in your life but we have to believe that there is going to come something more out of this than horrible migraines that kept you in a dark room all day." And yesterday, my daughter, Azalea, came home from school and she had tears in her eyes. And she said, "I found the answer why I have the concussion."

Seth: Oh my god, I just got goosebumps.

Sally: She won this major award from Disney because she wrote an essay about the experience with the concussion and what she had been doing while she was sitting in a dark room where she couldn't look at an iPad or a TV screen. She made lists of the random acts of kindness that she wanted to do for other people and she made a list of 100. And as soon as she started getting healthy, she executed this list. And so she wrote an essay about that and included the list. And Disney chose her essay as the one that is called Dreamers and Doers. And it's a parade and it's season passes for the whole family and a big award ceremony and everything. But I think that's a very personal example in my life. It's also true in business that sometimes things seem so hard and there's such a struggle and we bang our heads against the wall and think, "Why did I just lose that client? Why am I not able to make payroll right now at this time? Why did I lose that employee? Why can't I seem to grow and scale?" And it's only later that we can look back and see what was happening in the transformation. It's because we weren't able to see it. We were still in the process.

Seth: That is amazing. That is absolutely true and you've helped over half a million participants through the Fascination Advantage Assessment. What are you finding is the biggest mistake that people are making when they are trying to grow their businesses and be more fascinating?

Sally: People make a lot of mistakes because we're trained very badly on what the purpose of a personality assessment is and we have a lot of really bad habits. I'll give you an example. We often try to be better than our competition. You go after your competition's unique advantage and you try to outdo it. This puts you on this endless downward spiral of incrementally trying to outdo somebody else on what they already do best. And that's when we start to measure things like well, they're 0.82 KPI or whatever key performance indicator you want to pick and we're 0.81. So if we just try harder, we'll be better. What I propose is stop trying to be better and focus on being different. Different is better than better. And if you can identify something within your company, your product, your service, your employees, your team, yourself that is different even if it's a tiny difference and can seem insignificant but that difference can turn into a way bigger more scalable competitive advantage that gets you in a different playing field and attracts your ideal customer.

For example, when my last book came out, I decided that I wanted to incorporate professional speaking as part of my career, not as the basis of my company but as part of it. And so I looked at what other speakers were doing and I tried to be better than them. I tried to be more pulled together, seemingly more educated, well prepared. And in doing so, what I was doing was watering down my core traits that I could go on stage and build a relationship really quickly with the audience and show them a totally new way of seeing themselves. But in order for me to do that, in order for me to accomplish that goal, I can't try to emulate my competition. And so I was stuck. About three years ago, I was really stuck. My speaking fee had plateaued at an unimpressive level. And I just felt like I was working way too hard to try to make this work. And so I had to stop and stand back and say, "I need to stop trying to be better. I need to start being different in a way that's most authentic for me." And as soon as I did that, not only did my business explode, I was able to literally charge 1000 percent more for my speaking, 1000 percent fee increase in three years.

But I was inducted into the Speakers Hall of Fame which is the highest award that you could get in the speaking profession. There are only 200 people inducted in the whole world. And it also allowed me to create a business that works for my lifestyle so I can be home with kids when I need to. And so the biggest mistake is don't focus on your strength. Focus on being better. Strengths are commodities in a crowded competitive marketplace. Everybody has strengths. The question is, how are you different? And do like the greatest brands do. If you can identify what those differences are and then build your marketing around that and build your culture around that, you're going to be far more effective and have a more sustainable fulfilling business.

Seth: Different is better than better. I wrote that down.

Seth: Different is better than better. And you've obviously invented a way for everyone to find out not what makes them the same but what makes them different so that they can be better than better which is the Fascination Advantage Assessment. I've always wanted to know. It's such an amazing program. How did you come up with it?

Sally: What an awesome question. In the first half of my career, I was a copywriter for major brands like Coca-Cola, Target, Mini Cooper. I was part of the team that launched the Mini Cooper in the United States. When I was 24, I was the most award winning copywriter in the United States. When I was 27, I opened up my first advertising agency with clients like Target and Remy Martin. And when I was 31, my work was found in the Smithsonian Museum of American History. I love advertising. I love to find the perfect words to describe a brand and what it made most valuable. And what I found was in a headline or in a tag line or in body copy, in a sales letter, if you can find the perfect words to describe what makes a brand different, that brand can charge more money and it can attract a much higher level of consumer or customer or client that's willing to pay more and do more and refer more and stay loyal.

And about five years ago, I took some of the research that I've had, that I have done on what makes one company more fascinating than another. In other words, why is it that one company sells almost exactly the same thing as another but it can charge more money and it gets more of a cult following and gets people excited in social media. Why is that? What are the factors that trigger that? And I realized if I could take that same research and I could apply it individuals and that by taking the research that I had done, I could create a very different type of assessment that isn't measuring how you see the world. It's actually measuring the opposite. It's measuring how the world sees you at your best.

In other words, just as if Coca-Cola writes an ad, if they do a campaign that's about the delight and fun of the effervescence of the bubbles, then they're going to attract a certain type of customer and get a fairly predictable response. On the other hand, if they pay position it as a premium brand by hiring the hottest musician as a spokesperson, they're going to attract a different audience and get a different result. In the same way, I found that through a certain type of questions, I could use the same marketing algorithm that I had used to measure brands and I could apply it to individuals and measure what is that individual's most valuable traits, the qualities that people want to hire and promote and champion for and befriend. And then once it's identified, they can build the business around it.

So when you think of the Fascination Advantage, you can almost think of it like, imagine if you had a focus group of all your greatest fans, the best performance review you ever had, the friend who knows who you are inside and out, the partners you've had that you've gotten killer results for, if you think of how they would describe you at your best and then you took those descriptions and you turned it into marketing copy, that's what the report is. It's the marketing copy to describe who you are at your best so that you don't have to struggle when you're trying to figure out how to describe yourself in your website or trying to figure out at what direction you want to take your company in. It's all right there and it's been scientifically developed for individuals and teams to use based on my decade of research with half a million people.

Seth: And now, if I am correct, you are going back to what I would call your roots and the newest book that you're in the cave writing now is talking more about using examples of people who have done this for their companies. Am I correct? Can you expand on that?

Sally: In 2010, I released a book named *Fascinate: Your 7 Triggers to Persuasion and Captivation*. And *Fascinate* was really my initial work, my initial body of research on what makes one company or product or service more fascinating than another. But the book wasn't about individuals. It is about companies and it was also the first level, my first iteration of the Fascination System. It's version 1.0. It's like we can look back at an old iPhone and be like "well, that's clunky."

Then over the next four years, I shifted my research over to individuals because people kept coming up to me and saying, "What makes me fascinating?" And I found that when we measured individuals especially on a team or an organization that it became an incredible new data source, new information that people could see how they related to each other and their communications styles.

And it suddenly became very clear why there are communication breakdowns or conflicts or why people were quitting and why there was stoppage at certain areas such as the R&D department wasn't able to create innovation, wasn't able to come out with a new innovation because other people in that company were putting the brakes on it because they were so traditional. They just wanted to keep doing things the same way over and over. And so based on that realization, I wrote my last book which is *How the World Sees You*. And *How the World Sees You*, it's almost like a desk reference to everybody you know. It explains why your clients do what they do. It explains why your spouse charms you and irritates you at the same time. It's a very scientific look at personalities, deconstructing them according to their traits.

But then I looked back at the book I had done before that, *Fascinate*, the one we were talking about just a moment ago. And I realized that the system had evolved and we had done so much cool new work, pilot programs inside of companies and we had so many new juicy case studies that describe what happens when you create a culture of engagement that I needed to rewrite the last book. And I thought it was going to be one of those things where I was just doing cut and paste. For example, the innovation advantage which is all about creativity used to be named Rebellion because brands use Rebellion when they get you excited about that third slice of pizza or scoping Facebook when you shouldn't.

Seth: Yup. I was rebellion.

Sally: You were power and rebellion. Exactly. Which ultimately became the change agent in the new book. But I needed to go back and kind of re-jigger the whole last book. And I thought it would take me an afternoon. It turns out it took me, it's taken me about two months and it's been way more intense. Do you ever find, Seth, that rewriting something is sometimes harder than writing it in the first place?

Seth: All the time. Because you discover so much stuff that when you wrote it the first time you either didn't think of or know. In hindsight, that leads to rewriting that can almost lead to writing more than you did in the first place.

Sally: Right. We just bought a new house and we're decorating. And I'm bringing over the furniture from the other house. And I like the carpets fine and the chairs are fine. But then I want to replace the table but as soon as I replace the table, it was like "oh no."

Seth: Yup. Nothing else matches. And now, you might as well just scrap the whole thing.

Sally: Yeah. Now, we got to get rid of everything. Yeah, it's like –

Seth: You just got to live at Home Depot and the furniture store.

Sally: Yeah, yeah, yeah. I was joking with my editor that I thought that I was just, that I was altering a dress by hemming it. But what I really did is I turned the dress into a pantsuit. It's basically a new book. And that's kind of a blessing and a curse because it's still *Fascinate* but it is a much more practical pragmatic hands on way to be using this. What we found is every company has one primary language just like individuals but then they can use different tactics. And so this book is showing you step by step. Once you identify what your language is, then you can apply these different tactics based on the situation so that you can be targeting different types of people without being untrue to your macro positioning.

Seth: And you talk about not only applying Fascination to yourself to make it more fascinating or applying it to your company to attract the right kind of client but you also talk about using it internally with your team. Can you share a little bit more about that? That is fascinating as well.

Sally: When we went inside high performing companies and we looked at what the best employees were doing on their teams, we found some very interesting patterns. We found that great teams are not built on similarities. They're built on differences. They're built on personality diversity. In other words, if you have a team in which everybody is great at details, then balls are going to drop when it comes to inventing or evolving. So, one of our clients is a Fortune 100 Life Insurance Company. Their employees totally over index on the trust advantage which means they don't have a lot of employee turnover, their clients and customers tend to stay with them for a long time but they're really struggling attracting younger consumers and they don't have a great social media plan because they've just kind of stuck their head in the sand and they're ignoring that there is a revolution happening. That's a problem.

But alternatively, when we go and we work with startups and small businesses sometimes they score really high in innovation or prestige. So they're great at generating ideas. They can brainstorm all day long. They can come up with ideas but nobody is actually executing those ideas. You go in and you see all these Post It notes all over the walls and it looks like this amazing war room like something out of *A Beautiful Mind* but the ideas have never actually seen the light of day because nobody's implementing. And those are extreme examples. But on every team, if you're not identifying what people are already doing right and identifying those personal qualities they can leverage to add more value, to get better leads, to close the deal, then people are just following a one size fits all formula which is demoralizing and incredibly ineffective.

Seth: Absolutely.

Sally: Let me add on one last thing. So here's what we do. When we go into a team whether it's a small business or it's a solo entrepreneur who has two assistants or whatever setup you have – we've done this with 8000 people at a time. We go in and we measure everybody through the Fascination Advantage Assessment. Then we put the result on a heat map. If you can visualize a heat map, it's like – some people call it a scatter plot.

Sally: We're demonstrating how they cluster in certain areas and that certain traits are very, very prevalent within the organization and other ones might even be missing, nonexistent. And once the business leader, decision maker sees this visualization, it becomes so obvious why certain problems happen over and over again. And it also helps them position themselves to make sure that they're not a me too company. So if you know that you have really high use of power in your organization and you tend to hire, retain and promote people who have the power advantage, it's important for you to make sure that people have the opportunity to communicate your opinion and that the company is going to be opinionated. It will have a certain swagger to it if it's going to be a confident leader within the market. It shouldn't try to play small. It has to play big. And so we're talking before about how the assessment is based on marketing. What that means is you're going to apply all of this to the individual but you can ladder it up to the brand and to the direct selling and to the sales message that's going out to the community.

Seth: That makes a ton of sense. For our listeners who are resonating with what you're saying which I hope is everyone and who want to be more, who want to find out what makes them fascinating and how to use that to increase their success in business and in life, what is the ideal first step you want them to take? Where do you want them to go? What do you want them to do?

Sally: Well, we have a little secret surprise for them because, Seth, we are huge fans of yours. And we want to help you understand your audience but we also want your audience to be able to understand themselves better because this is a crucial part of them being more effective in their marketing and growing their business. So we're creating a complimentary code. And here's how to do it. Go to howtofascinate.com/you, howtofascinate.com/you and it will ask you for a code. And the code means that you don't have pay for it. It's complimentary. And the code is sethmagic, all one word, sethmagic, sethmagic.

Seth: Wow. You didn't tell me you're going to do that. Thank you so much. That is a huge gift for all of our folks. We greatly appreciate it. As always, speaking to you is well worth it and very, very reassuringly expensive. You get what you pay for. So I seem to remember a marketing campaign you did around that. So I greatly appreciate your time and the education you've been providing to our listeners about how to be more fascinating and how to use that on business and in life. It's been an absolute pleasure to pick your brain for half an hour. We greatly appreciate it.

Again, the website is howtofascinate.com/you and their promo code is sethmagic. To get your free Fascination Advantage Assessment, I urge you all to go do that as so that you can find out what makes you different so that you can be better than better. Thank you so much, Sally Hogshead for agreeing to share some of your wisdom with our listeners.

Sally: I love talking with you and I get so excited about this. And there's one last thing that I want to mention that people are invited to share this with their teams too because what makes you fascinating it's incredibly empowering and it's very strategic but the real power comes when you can understand the people around you so that you could tap into each person's differences. Remember different is better than better, right, Seth?

Seth: Yes. I've written it down. It must be true.

Sally: Cool. Thank you so much for having me join you. I appreciate it. I love talking to you.

Seth: Well. Thank you. I love talking to you. Thank you so much for the amazing information and the incredible offer you made to our readers.

26

BONUS MARKETING INTERVIEW WITH
ROLAND FRASIER

Seth: Today, I have the amazing good fortune to be interviewing one of my heroes in the industry, Mr. Roland Frasier who you probably already know from his amazing work at Digital Marketer with his partners, Ryan Deiss and Perry Belcher. His work leading their War Room Mastermind. Traffic and Conversion events, and serving an amazing portfolio of companies that are fortunate enough to be clients of theirs. Roland, thank you so much for joining us.

Roland: My pleasure, Seth. Thank you for having me.

Seth: We are happy to. Now, for those of our folks who don't know, you didn't start off as one of the top minds in marketing today. How did you get started?

Roland: When I was practicing law, I had the good fortune of dealing with a lot of entrepreneurial clients. And as the internet was coming into being, I had makeabet.com, betonit.com, nikonschool.com for photos, stuff like that. I did America Online, a channel in the motivational space. I did back in the CompuServe days, one of those guys in the beauty space. So lots of stuff online there. And then general Direct Response, I worked with Gary Halbert who is widely reputed to be one of the best copywriters. I did a lot of stuff with him. I did 16 infomercials, 14 with Guthy-Renker and 2 with K-Tel Direct and then a ton of direct mail. As a matter of fact, my direct mail company just turned 20 this year so I've been around for 20 years.

Seth: Happy anniversary.

Roland: Twentieth! Thank you. Yeah, it's pretty cool.

Seth: And how did you get to Digital Marketer?

Roland: Digital Marketer, it's really funny. I was just looking around in that space because I've done a lot of buying and selling of companies. And one of the biggest ways to add value to an existing company is to take people who are not marketing online and help them do that. And so, I saw Digital Marketer. I looked around the space at kind of all the different people who are in online marketing. And the people that really seemed to be consistently delivering the highest quality experience was Digital Marketer, Ryan Deiss, Perry Belcher. They have an event every year called Traffic and Conversion Summit. So I went to Traffic and Conversion Summit. So I think I may have gone to the second one. They have a high-end Mastermind called the War Room. And I ended up joining the War Room to get to know them and we ended up hitting it off and becoming friends. And ultimately when the opportunity arose to get to be part of the business, I bought.

Seth: Awesome! What do you wish you knew when you started that you know now?

Roland: Learning is incremental. So I would love to have started with all the things that I have learned since I started. I was talking to my wife about this the other day. The thing that I think is the most important across every business and online, it's especially important because we tend to be behind our computers a whole lot and not be out connecting with people. But almost everybody I know, the big money and the big success come from relationships. So I would have probably tried to form really strong relationships sooner and not tried to learn so much of how to write copy myself (although going down to Miami and sitting with Gary Halbert to show me how to write copy formed a relationship that ended up leading to other great relationships). But that required me getting out from my house, out from behind the computer, out from behind the pen and paper and actually talking to somebody. I'm sure that that would be the answer. I would have tried harder sooner to form those relationships. What do you think about that?

Seth: I think that's absolutely correct. I think that as you mentioned, a lot of us get stuck behind our computers looking at the latest Word Press plug-in or social network or app that's supposed to revolutionize our business or we may be working on a marketing plan but we don't have a people plan. We don't say, "Who are the ten most important people to the growth of Digital Marketer? And what is our people plan to build relationships and maintain those relationships and add value to the relationships with those folks?"

Roland: Exactly. And that's so important. And you're like that. I mean, I know. I've seen you out speaking at different Masterminds and things like that and those connections – in my experience, that's been the big, big leaps in every business. Even working with Digital Marketer and having this fantastic growth that we've had, some of our biggest growths have come from relationships that we formed with other people who have complementary audiences or services or access to people that we would like to have access to.

Seth: That segues perfectly into the question that you set me up for. So who are the five most, people external to Digital Marketer that would be most important to your growth?

Roland: We formed two relationships that I can talk about. One with InfusionSoft and one with click Bank that are relationships that really I think are key to us moving forward and fast. If you look at Digital Marketer several years ago versus now, it used to be very focused on kind of the latest thing, a little more business opportunity focused. Whereas now, it's much more focused on helping real businesses grow that exist already. To grow and train their staff and train their owners in the digital marketing field. And so as we've made that pivot, having relationships with the company like InfusionSoft that already has tens of thousands of the customers that we already want and allowing us to get in front of their customers and do it in a way that benefits them and also exposes us to their customers, that's a big deal.

I mean, that's exponential growth having those kinds of relationships and click Bank as well. Click Bank has I believe 600,000 publishers and over 200,000 affiliates. And so for us to form a relationship with click Bank where we're working together very, very closely, that's a big deal to us as well. As a matter of fact, I think it was a couple of months in to our relationship with click Bank that we went from doing no business with their affiliates to doing about half a million dollars a month. And that's just growing and growing and growing. So, those two would be significant. The others I cannot really talk about yet.

Seth: That's fair. You've had relationships with some of the greatest marketing thought leaders who are both living and who aren't with us anymore. Is there anyone on your business or marketing bucket list that you haven't had the chance to work with yet that you want to?

Roland: A really great question. I would love to do something with Elon Musk. I would love to do something with Richard Branson. I would love to do something with Warren Buffett. Those are all my bucket list. And you know what, every time you set your cap for something like that it seems like it ultimately works out. So I would advise doing something with those guys.

Seth: It's funny that I was driving through the bank today and I have never seen one before but there is a row of Tesla electric car charging station in the middle of a strip mall parking lot. Nothing else's there. There's no room for a Tesla dealership. I have no knowledge that there is one coming to Buffalo. I can't imagine there's enough money here to justify a Tesla dealership but perhaps they're just branding them Tesla. And they want more people to buy electric cars and charge at their station because if they charge them every day, they will aspire to one day own a Tesla.

Roland: Really? Yeah! I don't know. But you know, really funny, they have two Tesla charging stations at the Inn at Rancho Santa Fe. This is a small, little hotel. I don't even know if they're calling it a hotel. A small, little inn in the tiny little village of

Rancho Santa Fe where I live. So those things are popping up everywhere.

Seth: What with all that you've got going on and I can't even begin to imagine how busy you are, what is your biggest challenge?

Roland: Let me expand on the question before and then I'll answer this one if I may.

Seth: Of course.

Roland: The other thing that I think, rather than focusing for us on specific people, I do specifically focus on companies that I want to do business with. This year, we targeted Yahoo and Facebook and Sprint and several other companies to do business with. And in January, we were meeting with Sprint talking about a strategic relationship. In February and March, we met with Yahoo several times and we're moving forward with a show with Yahoo. I was at the Facebook brand new campus last month the day after it opened talking to their Director of Ad Products. And so it's really cool to me to be able to say we'd really like to figure out how to work with some of these companies who again have the kind of people that we want and are in the markets that we want to be in and then start developing relationships.

And one distinction there that I think is cool that might help your listeners is a lot of people are like "well, how do I do business with Yahoo?" Because Yahoo's huge. Do I just call 411 and say, "Can I have somebody at Yahoo?" For Sprint, the same way, right? What I found to be kind of a trend in us getting to know those companies and then expanding our network within them is that they usually have divisions within themselves that are smaller wholly owned subsidiary type companies. And so we went through a subsidiary of

Sprint that's funded by Sprint and answers to Sprint. But it's easier to get meetings at these little satellite companies.

So there was a company called Pinside I think is the name of it that was the Sprint subsidiary. And Yahoo has several divisions and several offices spread all over the place. And we were interested in doing videos with them so we met with their video division which is headquartered in Santa Monica. And same thing with Google right now, we're in the process of kind of winnowing our way through the YouTube division which is completely separate group of people (A) to get that relationship done but also that it can lead to other relationships. So these big companies that you want to deal with, you don't just have to know the CEO to do stuff. And they're not as hard to get to know if you just kind of look at where can you add value for them in a company that they own that then you can prove yourself and kind of move up the chain from there. Does that make sense?

Seth: It makes total sense. It's a great idea. And the second question was, what's your biggest challenge?

Roland: The biggest challenge we have is really there's so much opportunity and staying focused is tough because all of us get bored very, very quickly and we definitely have shiny new object syndrome. So we like to keep doing things that are new and take advantage of opportunities as they arrive. And if you say yes to everything, then you drown in opportunity and you never really finish anything. So our biggest challenge I think is balancing those opportunities with the ability to get them done. One of the big challenges there for us is in one of the evolutions of our doing new deals is that we've in the past taken on startups. We don't do startups anymore. We've in the past taken on companies or taken on an idea where there wasn't somebody in advance that we've identified that would run that division or run that project or whatever.

And so now, we don't take on any projects with what we call headless horses. It's a fantastic, amazing opportunity but we just don't have any personnel to staff it as a leader. If we don't have that, then we just say no. And we don't usually say no as much to great opportunities. We say not now and then we kind of try to find that person but we won't actually open up and dedicate resources to it unless we've got somebody to run it. Which leads to the corollary of that which is it's always challenging for us to find great people who share the visions of the different companies that we own internally and then have the work ethic and the motivation and the hunger to do as much as possible to make those divisions succeed because Ryan and Perry and I are very, very much dedicated to making everything that we do have very, very high quality customer experience, delivering more than we promise and really building value. And so finding people who have that inherent belief and also the hunger and desire to make that happen, to make things happen, that's a challenge for us, at least to find them in a quantity that we need to take advantage of the opportunities that we have.

Seth: That makes sense. You've had so many successes and so many amazing out of the park grand slam homeruns. I find sometimes we learn more from things that don't go as well. What has been your biggest mistake? And what did you learn from it?

Roland: Well, I'd say our biggest mistake in recent history has been that we start too many projects without having somebody to run them. So the learnings that I just mentioned come directly from – I think last year we spent at the beginning of the year maybe a million dollars or so on projects that we just didn't have somebody to head. And they kind of fizzled and so I think we would all like to have that million dollars back. But having learned from that pain of losing that, we have evolved to say we need heads on all of our horses.

And affiliate network-wise, last year, around January, we hired someone to help us with our affiliates. And between that person and another person who was out there in the market telling people "Hey, you can just sell this thing to these guys and you get paid this bounty and who cares if you give them crappy customers." We had – I don't know if you recall it, click fraud, but it's about as close to it as possible. We had a run where we lost, a million dollars. So we like to move forward fast, but those efforts to generate a whole lot of customers by going out into the customer acquisition market and then kind of having our hat handed to us to the tune of a million bucks. So we are much, much more careful about how we are going about our customer acquisition strategies through networks and things like that now as a result of that.

Seth: You mentioned shiny object syndrome and the constant changes going on in the marketplace. What do you do to stay on top of all of that information every month?

Roland: That's a really good question. I am a voracious consumer of all kinds of information. So I listen to audio books. I watch a ridiculous amount of video. I read a whole lot of blogs across multiple things from SEO to PPC to video marketing, to branding, to general marketing. I mean, it's just a passion so it's a really, really large amount of information being consumed. And to consume it, I use My Speed, which is a video accelerator, to watch videos at three times speed. I use the Podcast Speed Selection to listen to podcasts at least two times speed. And I use Spritz for all the blogs that I read to be able to read the blogs super, super fast. So all of those ways to compress, consuming that information into as little time as possible sure helped me to continue to have a quality of life outside of business.

Seth: Absolutely! Jimmy Vee and Travis Miller who I know you know just shared a tip with me at a recent super conference about how they buy the audio version of the physical book, then they buy the physical book too and then they read the physical book while listening to the audio version at like two and a half times speed because just listening to it at two and a half times speed you cannot necessarily grasp it all. But if you listen to it while you read it, you can read through it really, really fast.

Roland: That sounds interesting! Most of my listening is done like either while I work out or while I'm on an airplane. Usually, I've got something else going on at the same time so that I'm probably not getting as much of it as I should but that sounds like a great idea. For me, I don't really find that much new and evolutionary or that's helpful to me in evolving my thinking. It's not that often that it happens but it might be one idea or two ideas in the entire book. And so going through it super, super fast gets me get through all the filler. And then when I get to the parts that actually have some meaning, I will slow it down to normal speed and listen to it. And then I'll typically listen to it two or three times.

Seth: What are three of the best books you've ever read that have had the most impact on your work? And you can't quote something that you wrote.

Roland: Let me just give you a couple of recent ones because those classics have all had tremendous impact, all the ones that you already know from *The Robert Collier Letter Book* and Caples and Ogilvy, Eugene Schwartz to Dale Carnegie and Napoleon Hill. Those were all kind of – hopefully, everybody says those. Recently, I really enjoyed reading, Diamandis' book which I think is called *Bold* and also Peter Thiel's, *Zero to One* and then the revised *Blue Ocean Strategy* were all books that I've read recently. If I was going to pick three that I really enjoyed and got a lot out of recently, I would say those.

Seth: Terrific! Great recommendations! We greatly appreciate your time. We know how valuable it is. For our listeners who are resonating and loving everything you're saying and who want more from Roland Frasier and Digital Marketer, where will be the best place for us to send them? Do you want them to go straight to digitalmarketer.com? Or do you want us to send them someplace else?

Roland: Well, digitalmarketer.com has a tremendous amount of fantastic marketing information. I'm on Facebook. It's facebook.com/RolandFrasier. On LinkedIn and Twitter under that same name. So I think if you want me specifically, then those are good places. If you want all of us together and all the cool marketing stuff that DM is doing, then definitely digitalmarketer.com. And DM Lab, I think, is $38 a month.

Seth: Yes. It's a no brainer. But I'm a huge fan and love the content you guys put out all the time. It's very helpful.

Roland: Cool! Well, thank you very much.

BONUS MARKETING INTERVIEW WITH
WILL DUQUETTE

Seth: I have the great fortune to be here today with Will Duquette. Will, welcome.

Will: Hey, thank you for having me. Appreciate it.

Seth: You are very welcome. I'm going to take you back in time a little bit and I know you've got an incredible journey that you've been on over quite a long period of time. I'm going to ask you how did you get started.

Will: I was taught stuff like 'work hard to get ahead.' I was working two and three jobs and I barely had any money and definitely had no life. So that didn't work out and then I went to college, where I realized kind of quickly within that means that wasn't going to get me rich. It was just going to get me a job and if I was lucky, a high paying job, so I was like, "Okay, that's not really the route to go."

I tried every single get rich quick scheme on the planet looking for a way to build wealth. It wasn't until I went to a non-conventional seminar where it taught me real estate investing, with no money down, no credit and stuff like that. So now, I have my two businesses because I went out and learned by buying books, real estate courses and seminars and learning from people who have been there and done that. Really just studying how did the people who were poor might end up one day become rich. I just went and started to apply it so that's the short version of it.

Will: I was a bar tender for many, many years. I was a handy man. So I used to do all kinds of things and I was trying to get rich and make money and change my life and my world. For the last job that I ever had in my life and I called in with walking pneumonia with a doctor's excuse and they fired me anyway .

It made me mad enough to realize that I'm never been in charge, I'm never going to get wealthy unless I actually take charge of it and go out and create my own business.

So I really just said "Okay, I'm going to start my own business," and lawn care is something I liked to do at that time back then. I went on and started my own lawn care service. Six months later, I was making more money doing that part-time just three days a week and I did that on my own terms. I worked with who I wanted too. I could actually create my own income.

Six months later, I'm doing well, making money but then I still had a job. I went on and got my real estate license to teach me how to do real estate investing but it definitely did not teach me that all. But it did teach me the legalities of it and I was shown basically how to get another job.

I wanted to actually learn how to buy and sell real estate as a net investor and make a 100 percent commission rather than three percent commission. I was literally still bartending one night part-time and I had my own lawn care service during the day, doing pretty well.

I went into a real estate investing seminar to kind of just check it out and see what they're doing. And there was a guy on stage that promised to teach us all how to make money with no money down, no real estate license needed and without needing any credit to go build wealth. Make hundreds of thousands and even millions of dollars was his promise if we just bought his book, courses and seminars to the tune of $7,500 and that was 17 years ago. Well, that scared the heck out of me.

I didn't know anybody who had $7500 back then. I had one credit card with a $10,000 limit on it and at first I was afraid to go forward and actually purchase that stuff but then ultimately, it was a turning point for me at that point because a waitress at that time said, "Hey, let's go there and check out what the guy has going on down there in the seminar room because I know that your license didn't work out".

So I went down the room kind of apprehensively and it's amazing that sometimes we meet people in life and they'll say something or do something and it will change the entire rest of the course of our life or a perspective of our lives. And this waitress changed my course because I came back to the bar and she said, "Well, what's going on?" I said, "Well, it sounds great. But my God, he wants to sell this thing for $7500". And she said, "Oh, my gosh," I said, "I know that's crazy." I never bought anything for 7 grand unless it's a car and I finance that.

And so, she said innocently enough, so now what are you going to do? You know, I did not purchase at that time. I really sit back and ponder the rest of that night, it just bothered me. And I said, you know what, she is right. What am I going to do? Am I going to keep bartending, keep the lawn care service, or am I going to actually take a little bit of risk, you know, really swing for the fence and make this a go. He showed me here's what's happening. He showed me testimonials and he showed me how the students are doing it. Showed me it was possible and yet there was one core emotion that keeps me and most people from getting everything that they want and that's fear because there's really two core emotions, love and fear. When I really understood this, I said okay I've got to get past my fears.

I went down the back on the seminar room and I really pulled out my credit card and I mean literally I said "Am I insane here I can't believe I'm going to do this." I spent $7500 on my credit card. I had to fly off to Seattle, Washington twice for the next two boot camps that he was having within the next few months which obviously maxed out my credit card.

Well, what that did for me is it set me aside from the normal person. Literally in the moment that I signed stating that I'm buying this thing for $7,500, the moment that I did that it literally had me a mindset shift from "I'm not one of the paupers anymore". I had a shift but I didn't know it at the time but I know now I had a shift from a pauper mentality over to a millionaire's mentality. Because a millionaire's mentality is, "How can I do it?"

Now, a millionaire mindset I understand is, "Yes, here is what I want, no excuses but how can I do this," and I actually went forward in that motion. Again, not even knowing that I was doing this and that was a major that was actually, very first huge turning point in my life to financial freedom was actually commit to spending that money and really putting myself on the line taking another risk saying, here's $7,500 to give me this. And I'm investing in myself to go make money in real estate and trusting this other people to say that what this is, it will work and I knew nothing about real estate investing.

I went to the first seminar, they gave me their home study courses. I started applying it. I failed forward fast and what happened for me was I spent 10 grand basically with no exit strategy other than this has to work or I don't have 10 grand to pay the credit card companies back, period. That was just the way it was.

I remember over the course of a couple of years of going to trainings, I'd see similar people at the same seminars. I remember this one guy in particular that I knew very well. He was from the same town that I was from. And I started going up on stage and sharing some of my success stories, some of those real estate deals that I was doing. And I had to learn a whole new language pattern around real estate, not only real estate, but also about becoming wealthy, becoming a millionaire.

So this shift would be one, of commitment, and two, learning a whole new language and three, learning a new mindsets about who it is I'm going to be in the world. What am I going to commit to do? And on top of it, take the action. Even in the face of fear, that's the biggest key. There's going to be fears, there will be challenging times and you have to say, "Here's who I am. Here's what I'm going to achieve". Make a statement for it. Put it out there and this is what I'm going to do and take whatever comes your way and this tenacity like I'm just going to make it happen. And so, that's what I did.

Three or four years later, I met a guy who asked me, you know, he saw me go up on stage and he says, "Hey, what are you doing? How are you doing this?" Oh yes, great. I got this deal going on, I did this over here. I made 30 grand over there and made $70,000 with this deal and made this over there. And I remembered him saying to me and I remember being in complete puzzlement when he asked me the question.

He said to me, "Oh my God. Will, that's awesome. How did you do that?"

And I remembered looking at him like, "Wait a second, you went to the same seminars I went to".

Will: You had the same training courses I have. The first thing that popped in my mind is how did you not do it? They spelled out for you exactly what to do and it was my first glimpse of most people say they want to be rich; most people say they want wealth. They're not willing to risk what they have in order to achieve that. I set a new goal and a new milestone for myself even today. Here's what I'm going to create in the next three, four, five years and I'm willing to bet it all. Roll the dice. "I'm putting all my chips in on this".

This is what I'm doing and so, I have no exit strategy just like with the $10,000 when I first started. And every time I create something new, that's because I've risked a huge chunk of it. When I start playing that way, I stop thinking small and I have no plan B. I think I saw an interview with Will Smith one time, and he talked about this. He says, "There is no plan B. Its plan A and that's what is going to happen. Hell or high water, that's what I'm doing," and like that's what it really takes. And most were not willing like really put themselves out there like that. They're afraid of looking bad. Well, one of the things this guy did not want to do is that "we buy houses" on his car - a car sign. You got people probably seeing them around town. And so, I just did it, right?

Even in the face of people making fun of me, what is that? You look silly with that sign and all that stuff. So you got to stop worrying about what other people think, you've got a choice. You can either make friends or you can make wealth. You can either get along and do what's popular, or you can do whatever it takes in order to build wealth. And the crazy thing is as soon as you start making money, all who I thought were my friends started disappearing not because I thought I was better than them, really because they felt insignificant and they left then. And they realized that I was just on a different space and I even try to encourage many of them.

I said, "Hey, come over here, I'll show you what I'm doing. I'll show you how to get there," and that guy still to this day is working a JOB and never really hit the milestones that he wants to and since then, stopped contacting me. He doesn't want to hang out with me. It's been many, many years.

Now, were talking 17 years later, since then I've gone out to the next milestone which is I want to be a motivational speaker. I want to be a person who trains other people. I want to have two businesses - real estate investing as well as educating other people, giving this information.

So now, I have two businesses - one is in information business and I also learned how to be a hypnotist. How to have persuasion and influence skills. Well, I don't know how stronger you can be to actually have the powers of being a hypnotist and how to speak to people on a subconscious level.

I remember every six months, I used to feel like I had to pinch myself. I made so much money, my first deal in real estate, I made $17,600 and it took about two or three hours of work time and I couldn't believe it. I was like, "Oh my gosh, this is amazing". It used to take half a year to make that much money. And so every six months, I made so much money I couldn't believe it. It was like a dream. And that's great that we have success and what I had figured out along the way is I still wasn't happy. Like I made money and it was great and I could make my bills, but I still didn't have great relationships.

I started getting out of shape. I was getting fatter and I was just wasn't happy. I'm really thinking, "How in the world could I have ten times the income I used to have and yet I still feel the same exact way about myself and about life and relationships?"

That's how I get into personal development seminars. I got into being a hypnotist and learning about how to be happy in the inside as well as having enough income on the outside. And what I realize is I to shift from what I called success to significance.

And that's why I live today within a space of significance. Every single day, I change people's lives. Every single day I'm doing what I'm doing right here on this call with you. I mean there's people who are going to listen to this and be motivated and inspired. Because I can tell you right now, I'm not a genius, I'm not a super book smart guy. I used to think I kind of dumb. I was picked on as a child. I was told I was a retard. I was told I had learning disabilities. I was told I would never amount to nothing.

Every single person within the sound of my voice here is amazing beyond potential. The challenge is most people are not willing to lay themselves on the line to really risk it and say, "You know what, I am amazing". Give yourself permission to do it. I grew up in a public school system, and we were taught stuff like, "Don't brag, don't be known always want to win, don't be the one that's always winning," you need to have a champions mentality like Tiger Woods or somebody like Donald Trump. I've been on stages with Donald Trump that he's been on Sir Richard Branson. You name the names and now here I am, a guy that can barely spell and my penmanship is horrible. Here I am speaking and being around the top thought leaders of the world.

But what happened for me is that I realized that they're not special, right? Donald Trump is not amazing beyond belief. Anybody on the call at all, if their father gave them 200 million dollars to go out and invest in real estate. Any single person right now could take that 200 million dollars and within a reasonable amount of time, go out and turn it into 900 million dollars worth of debts which is comical but that's exactly what Donald Trump did.

And when I met him, he talked about that conversation. What I realized is that we are all smarter than Donald Trump. He makes mistakes and has challenges too. He was 900 million dollars in debt, where is he now? Back on top, why? Because his brain, the subconscious mind tells him so. See, Donald Trump didn't grew up with a pauper's mentality. He grew up with a millionaire's mentality. Now, none of us had the challenge of being front page news of the world. News companies saying, "Donald Trump is broke to the tune of 900 million dollars negative."

None of us have that pressure. Yeah, he shared me a story at that time that he said that he was invited to a cocktail party that same exact week that that front headlines came out. And he said I had a choice and this is where it really sets you apart. He said I had a choice of going to the cocktail party or not because obviously, how good is it and you feel about this so everybody knows. And then on top that, he said that 80 percent of the money that was owed at 900 million dollars, those investors were going to be at this cocktail party.

Now, this is what I going to share with you, the difference between a pauper's mentality to a millionaires' mentality. Because Donald Trump said, "Hey, as much as I didn't want to go to the cocktail party I knew that hey, I got to go face this thing and I will deal with this. I'm not going to go away. I'm not going to ignore it". A pauper mentality - ignore it and it will go away, don't deal with it, if it's a problem, run away from it, et cetera. Us millionaires, we realize that there's a problem, there's money to be made around a problem because how do you build wealth? Look for a problems and come up with the solution.

So he said he went to this cocktail party and, of course, the first thing to happen is this investor sees him, "Come here Donald, let's sit down and talk. What's going on?" He said it was the smartest move he ever did because they sat down, came up with a business plan and they shared with him the strategy, how to get back out of this, so he could create the income to pay them back. Additionally, they discounted down how much he actually owed them if he paid it off on a certain amount of time so gave him a goal to go to do that.

Had he not gone to the cocktail party that could have never happened.

In fact, I'm holding in my hand a list of the notes that I took when I was speaking to him about what was important on how to build the wealth. And I literally keep it to this day on my desk as a constant reminder.

When I've seen Donald Trump, really within 15-20 minutes, I realized he had a worthiness issue. Well, think about it, his dad was very, very successful. He lived in a shadow of this guy. So he'd have all these stories going on and then he actually validated it by telling and sharing with us the whole group that was there, that he actually enjoys golfing with what he calls "losers" so that he feels good about himself.

And when he shared that with me I thought what an awesome guy to come and share with us, his true feelings in the inside. "Hey, you know what, we all have those feelings and it's completely natural". It's completely okay. And the challenge is we never give each other a break because we're not told that it's okay to make mistakes. Mistakes are nothing more than learning lessons.

Seth: Let me ask you this, I know you are a voracious reader and a lifelong learner. Quickly, what are the three best books you've ever read that has had the most impact on your life and you can't quote the Bible or something you wrote yourself?

Will: Well, top of the line is *Think and Grow Rich*, right. I think anybody who's ever built wealth has had to have that. If you don't have that - that is literally the Bible of building wealth. *Think and Grow Rich* is going to be the top one for me and then the rest. The other one's are really going to be around what industry that you want to go into.

Seth: For folks on our list who want more from Will Duquette. What is the best place for them to go to learn more about you and what you can do?

Will: Well, they could go to willpowerduquette or just willduquette. com. Just go to my website, check me out. See what you need where I can I help you with. Plenty of resources there for them and to get in contact with me and I can help you with whatever way they need.

Seth: Okay, thank you so much.

Wow, that was a lot of great content from some amazing Podcaster's and Marketers. I hope you got as much out of it as I did.

So now that you have hopefully been inspired as to what a Podcast can do for you, it's time to take the next step of implementation. Where the rubber meets the road.

If you have a Podcast already, I will show you how to make it better. If you don't have a Podcast, I will show you how to create one even if you don't know what a Podcast is.

Are you ready? Good, let's get started.

So if you took nothing else away from the previous chapters of the book, here are the three "writer downer's" I want you to know:

A Podcast will help you get in front of impossible-to-reach decision makers and get them to seek you out. It will help you to write a book without actually having to write a word of it, which is very helpful (and it's how I wrote most of this book) It will get you customers for your business, from iTunes for as little as $15 a month. Sound good?

So why Apple? Why iTunes? Why a podcast? Apple is the leader in digital media distribution. They have customers in over 120 countries. They are the largest keeper of treasure trove of credit cards ever. There are over a billion subscribers to podcasts. So you can get your audio or video podcast in Apple really easily and we're going to teach you step-by-step exactly how to do that.

So what is a podcast to start with? Think of it as the new media version of a radio show or a TV show. Now, the majority of podcast are audio and that's where I'm going to suggest you start. You can do a video podcast. There are fewer people watching video podcasts and a lot more people listening to audio podcast. Because think about it, if you're running on a treadmill, if you're at work, it's much easier to just have your headphones and then listen to something than it is to watch. It's a lot harder to multi-task watching something and doing something else at the same time.

So it's really exciting when you think about the fact that only 25% of the world has a smartphone. And over the next three years, it's going to flip. So think about 25 percent of the world has a smartphone, 75 percent do not. By 2020, 75 percent of the world will have a smartphone, 25 percent will not. So the amount of people that you will be able to reach is going to triple.

So (a) three times as many people will have smartphones, and (b) everyone who buys a car in the next five or so years, even if they don't have a smartphone, will have a smart car. So it's massive market penetration.

So go to: http://www.ultimatemarketingmagician.com/ podcasts and check out my podcast. I would also love it if you would give me a 5 star rating and a great review. That's one of the secrets to getting your Podcast out there – ratings and reviews.

My Podcast called Direct Response Marketing. It is called that for a reason specifically because I am trying to rank for the keyword Direct Response Marketing. So that's one of the things we're going to teach you, is how to title your podcast because the app store has its own search engine optimization that you can do to try and rank your podcast for a specific keyword. So mine is ranking.

You have a voice like a radio show personality. So it helps people get to know, like and trust you better. I've had people talk to me and say, "Oh, my God. I feel like I know you already." And I've never had a conversation with them but they've listened to my show. It can help make you a celebrity in your niche and help you differentiate yourself.

So the steps to your podcast. First it needs a name. Then you need to write an introduction and your introduction is two to three minutes, a little bit of a bio, who you are, what the podcast is, what's it about. You're going to script your interview questions. The most popular podcasts are in interview style. You interview somebody else.

My favorite non-interview podcast is, you should all listen to it – it's called Warrior On Fire. It's by Garrett White, who's a friend of mine and an amazing entrepreneur and his is every day. Mine is not every day but his is. He rants for five to ten minutes on a topic of the day. So it's inspirational. In order to monetize your podcast the way we're going to show you, you want to be an interview show. The interview is designed to make them look good, make them feel good about you and let you show off a little bit, and drive more business.

You want to book your first guest. Then you can record the interview in a bunch of different ways. There's a million different software programs. You could Skype. You could GoTo webinar. I use an app called Call Recorder in iPhone. It's free. You just pay for the minutes of recording time. You're going to record your interview. We're going to get you an intro. There are a bunch of different software programs that you can use to upload your podcast to iTunes.

We'll show you how to sign-up for one of them and show how to use it. You upload your first episode. You tell iTunes to go get it and then you repeat. So, those are the steps and now let's go into all of that.

How to name your podcast. The first thing you want to do is start searching iTunes for the most successful podcast in your niche and name yours something similar. No copyright infringement. You can't copy them. You can't say this is the Nike Golf podcast.

So you want to search the podcast app in iTunes and search for what would people be looking for about you. Are they searching for podcast on X? Is there podcast already on that topic?

So you want to find the one that shows up number 1 and see what they are doing. What is their podcast name? What is their description? How many reviews do they have?

So you can see that the #1 Personal branding Podcast is Called:

Life is a marathon: life coaching – Self-Esteem – Personal Development – Personal branding – Positive Thinking

You see how he put his keywords in his title? You want to do that too.

If you click on ratings and reviews you will see he has 92 ratings, 88 of which are 5 star ratings. He's doing great. That's part of why he's #1.

You can also use Google's keyword tool. Google Keyword Planner is a free tool that will let you see what people are searching for online on the web because ultimately this will help you rank your website for whatever keyword you're trying to rank for.

So google keyword planner is telling us the monthly trends of the keyword searches. Personal branding and it's related keywords got 1.8 Million searches in May, but dropped to 1.4M in July and August. Maybe people care less during the summer. I don't know.

Personal branding itself got 22,000 searches a month. "Personal branding tips" got 720. So if I were trying to start a podcast around personal branding, I might want to start there.

So, you want to do research both in iTunes and in Google.

Your introduction should be a lead-generation ad for your podcast and the next action you want them to take after listening to it. So mine gives a brief bio of me. It talks about what we're going to do on the podcast.

"Welcome to the Direct Response Marketing Magic Podcast. Seth Greene is a 5-time best-selling author, speaker and nationally recognized direct response marketing expert who is CEO of one of the fastest-growing direct response marketing firms in the country. To get free access to his magical marketing video series that will show you how to attract new customers like magic, simply register at www. ultimatemarketingmagician.com. On the podcast, Seth brings together some of the most cutting-edge thought leaders in the world to share with you how they grow their businesses and how you can, too. And now, here's your host, Seth Greene."

So even if hypothetically they did not listen to the episode, if all they heard was the first two minutes, they've been driven to my site. And your bio should be written in such a way that it positions you as the expert in the niche. Gary Occhino is the U.S. Junior National Team Coach and the number 1 amateur golf coach in the country.

Interview questions. So these are some of my interview questions and you can just fill in the blanks. So this was for my last book, Cutting-Edge Marketing Magic, which was also an interview book.

I interviewed 15 of the top marketers. I transcribed the interviews; that was the book. These were marketing people.

So my first question was, "How did you get started in marketing?" How did you get started in, sales? How did you get started in – so if I were interviewing home improvement contractors, "How did you get started in being a home improvement contractor?" Remember everybody loves – this is a chance for them to talk about themselves and everybody loves to talk about themselves.

So you want to get them to tell their story because podcasts are all about storytelling. What story are you telling with this episode? And it's the person's story that you are interviewing. Sometimes people go from one firm to another, so I've said how did you get to this particular firm or this particular business? If they address this in how did you get started, then I don't ask it. If they say, for example we're doing a podcast for an estate-planning attorney, and we're interviewing his centers of influence. So we're interviewing financial advisers, CPAs, nursing homes, people who serve his target market. So the financial adviser, if he says," I went straight from out of high school and never left", then I'm not going to say, "How did you get to this particular firm?" You've got to sort of improvise a little bit.

This is one of my favorite questions. "What do you wish you knew when you started that you know now?" Everybody laughs. And then they go, "Wow, that's a really good question. I'll think about it for a minute." And they come up with something really good, which you can really learn from – your listeners are learning from, you're learning from and they get a chance to feel good about themselves. I will say – sometimes if they mention something – when I say what do you wish you knew, sometimes they will reference something they didn't do correctly and I will say, "You know that's interesting that you brought that up," because I sort of scripted it to get to that point, so I find our listeners often learn more from people's failures than their successes. What's your biggest mistake and what did you learn from it?

So they're designed to sort of segue into each other. They'll talk about a mistake they made, and I'll say, "Yeah, that makes sense" or "Wow, I can't believe you went through that. Now that you've gotten through that, what's your biggest challenge today?" This is a design to probe for pain question.

What's your biggest challenge? They're going to say, "Jeez, I want to market my business better. I'm having trouble keeping up with everything. Whatever their pain-point is, because then I will address that when the episode is over. Say, "Oh, you did mention that you're having trouble growing your presence on social media,." Through the marketers I ask them what their most successful marketing campaign was, this gave them a chance to show off and generate interest in it for them for the people listening, but it also gave me a lot of great ideas. They said, "Oh, that's really a good idea. We should do that, too."

What's your most cutting-edge, magical marketing idea? That was the name of the book that these interview questions for, it's cutting-edge marketing magic. So I was looking for what was the sexy new thing they were doing which taught me stuff I wasn't doing.

"How do you stay on the cutting-edge?" I will preface this with – we're bombarded with information. You see 5,000 messages a day. How do you stay on top of it all? They'll say things like – this is going to be different depending on the business, but I've gotten people who'll say, "I'm in a mastermind group." People who have recommended apps that they use, like Zyte, which allows you to create your own magazine, have only articles that interest you, only topics that interest you and every day you go click on it and it refreshes and gives you new content, which is really cool. I learned about that by interviewing somebody.

What do you read each month? I find this really interesting because they will tell you the trade journals and periodicals that they read and the magazines that they get and the newsletters that they're on. So it's great for doing market research because if I was interviewing a home improvement contractor, I don't know the home improvement magazines. I'm going to Google it and say "home improvement contractor magazine" and find a couple, but I'm not going to know the search terms and they'll tell me what they read, which will allow me to go get copies of those magazines and then see what they're like.

You don't have to ask this question. I ask, "What are the three best books you've ever read that had the most impact on your work?" And my little joke after that is you're not allowed to cite the Bible or a book you wrote yourself. Everybody laughs. That's a great question. Let me turn around and look at my bookshelf. You mean I have to narrow it down to three? And then they pick. Every single book that I haven't read that someone has mentioned I have bought because I am a voracious reader and it's a really great way to find books you never would have thought of. Like the guy on the interviewing Japan podcast happened to mention three books I knew I had read already, but I had a person the week before, the founder of wellness.com referenced books that were health and wellness books that I never would have thought to read. Apparently everything we eat is bad for you. Enjoy your lunch.

And then I'll say, "Hey, what makes you different from other firms that do what you do?" this is their chance to talk about why they're different and then my last question is "Hey, for our listeners that are resonating with you, they want to learn more, what's your podcast that they should subscribe to or what books they should buy or what's your website or where can they go to learn more about you? It's the chance for the interviewee to plug themselves. Afterwards they all say, "You gave me the opportunity to self-promote, awesome." I said, "Well, that's my business, but okay."

I got 21 podcasters to agree to the interview, and these were the questions I asked them. I said, "How did you get started in podcasting?" Noticed I changed it from marketing to podcasting. I asked this selfish question for myself, "How many downloads or subscribers do you have?" Because the person who had 500 subscribers, honestly I care less about than the guy who has one million subscribers.

Question for the folks reading the book who want to know how to grow a podcast, I asked, "How are you growing your listener base?" Because everybody does it differently. Some guy locks on to iTunes New and Noteworthy in the first week and all of a sudden has 20 thousand downloads. Other people, it takes more time. So, iTunes, the app has a section called New and Noteworthy where Apple will put podcasts it recommends and there's a whole process in how you get your podcast to show up in New and Noteworthy that I just learned that I will be working on to get ours to show up there. Because when you show up in New and Noteworthy, that's showing up on the homepage of everyone who's looking for app for a podcast and you get gigantic exposure.

How do you select and find your guests? Because people who are starting a podcast I surveyed and found out that podcasters view this as a really big challenge. "Oh my God, how am I going to get someone to be on my show when I have no listeners yet? Nobody's going to return my call or my e-mail. How am I going to get people to be on my show?"

We solve that problem for you and we're going to train you in a few minutes on how we solved it. But I wanted to see how other people were doing it, because I didn't want to assume that my way was the right way. It's not. It's just another way. Then I asked the capitalist question, "How are you monetizing your podcast?" Because we're doing this hopefully to make money. There are a lot of different ways to monetize your podcast. You can have a free version and a premium version. So iTunes will let you – you can charge for it and Apple will pay you. Someone says, "I want to buy this for $0.99 or $2 or $5. They pay Apple and you get money.

You can monetize your podcast by selling ads on it. You got a radio show. How do radio shows make money? Advertising. I wouldn't necessarily do that when you have one listener. It might be a more attractive proposition to sell advertising when you've got a good following. You can sell sponsorships. Someone could be the sponsor of an episode or they could be the sponsor of the entire show, an entire season, and most importantly, it should drive business. I asked again, "What do you wish you knew when you started? What's your biggest mistake? What's your biggest challenge? How do you stay on the cutting edge? What do you read every month? What are the three best books you've ever read? And what makes you different from other firms or podcasters or whatever it is that you're doing?" So those are my interview questions as you'll see in the book when you get it.

How do you get guests to be on your show? Especially if you are brand new and have no listener base?

It's easier than you might think.

The first step may seem simple, but you need to determine who it is that would deliver the biggest benefit to your guests, and increase the reach of your show (those may be two different types of guests).

Here's is an example. I recently interviewed Digital Marketer's Roland Frasier on my Direct Response Marketing Podcast. As one of the top marketing minds in the country, Roland has a huge following. However, Roland does not have a Podcast at this moment (I'm working on that). So while he was very generous to Facebook post his appearance on my show, and he delivered great content to my listener base, it didn't have the biggest impact in increasing my listener base.

On the other hand, I interviewed Joel Bogess of the ReLaunch Podcast. Joel has over 500,000 subscribers to his Podcast. So when he promoted that he did my show, and when he had me on his show – I immediately saw a dramatic spike in new subscribers and listeners to my show. I'm not knocking the amazing content Joel shared, but he had more of an impact on my show because he has one as well.

Do you see the difference?

No how do you get folks like that to be on your show?

Are you ready?

Ask. Well, you have to do a few things before you ask. You should always deliver value first, and become a part of their community. So if they have a podcast, subscribe to it. Listen to it. Rate it 5 stars and write a great review. Publicize it on your social media. Take screen shots of all of those things, and then email it to your desired guests. Tell them how much you liked a certain episode they did, and what it meant to you. Then reference how much your audience would benefit from something similar.

That's all there really is to it, most folks are very generous with their time and are willing to help.

There are also hundreds of Facebook and Linked in Groups of Podcasters that you can join, and if your target guest isn't in the group, chances are that someone in the group will know how to get to them.

Now let's talk about recording the interview. I personally use the Call recorder app. This is the one I use. Again, you could use Skype. You could use Go To webinar. You could use anything else. There's no right answer. If you go in your phone and you go to the app store and you type call recorder, there'll be a whole bunch of call recorder apps that come up.

This is the one you want, at least in my opinion. It is free. You download it and all you pay for is the minutes of recording time, and they're really cheap. You can get hours and hours and hours for a couple of bucks.

Here's how you use it. You click the Record button. It calls the service and then you hit Add Call and add the call to the person that you're taping, that you're interviewing. And then you hit, I'm picking them as a contact. I put them in my phone. I dial them and then you hit "Merge Calls" and then you record it. So what I do is I will call the person, "Hey are you ready for your interview. Here's what's going to happen. I'm going to interview you. We're going to transcribe it and edit it and give it to you for your approval before we put it in the book. And if it's okay with you, I'd also like to air it on my podcast to get you more exposure." "Yes, that would be great." "Okay. I'm going to hit the Record button. I'm going to ask you some questions you could answer in your sleep that are going to make you look good. At the end, I'm going to say, "Thanks for doing the interview. You're going to say thanks. I'm going to hang up. Then I'll call you back and we'll talk about it." And they say, okay.

So those first minute where I talk to them of what I'm going to do, it's recording blank space until you hit Merge Call, it's not actually recording them. So I will just have my audio editor edit out the minute of blank space and replace it with my intro, the professionally produced happily sounding intro. So that's the Call Recorder app. A couple of steps, it's free. You just pay for the minutes. It's very easy.

You want your professionally recorded intro, so that it sounds like a real radio show. The recorder app at the end when you're done, it will say, you have a new call recording available. You e-mail it to yourself and download the MP3 file on your computer and you now have your episode. You have to do two things with it. You need to put your intro on it. So if you're doing the done-for-you service, just e-mail us your MP3 and we'll do it for you. If you're doing this yourself, you can get Audacity which is a free audio editor where you just take the MP3 file of your intro and your episode, and it's like a word doc. You cut, you paste and it seamlessly transitions. And it takes minutes.

There are other free audio editors. Audacity's the top one and the one we would use if we were doing it. You can just Google free Audio Editor.

And then now you need to get it to iTunes. So you're going to sign-up for Libsyn. Now there are a bunch of different content aggregators that submit to iTunes, hundreds of them. I haven't looked at all of them. I've looked at the top four or five. Libsyn happens to be the one I use. You can use whatever you want, but I'm going to walk you through Libsyn.

So you want to sign-up at www.Libsyn.com. The steps are pretty simple – I would start at either Libsyn Classic 250 or Libsyn Advanced 800.

Here is how to start your show the first time. First you have to register a new show.

Your Show Slug should be your show name, then you fill out your credit card info and which option you want.

Next you want to edit show settings. Your show description is what people will see on your Podcast's page on Itunes. You want to make sure to tell them why they should listen to the show, what they will learn, and who you are. Once that is done then you need to upload your first episode before you submit to Itunes.

Next is how to upload an episode: Go to content and pick add new episode.

Your media file is the mp3 you made. Title is the tile of the episode. Subtitle is what the episode is about. Description is the bio of your guest, what they are talking about, and your bio. Thumbnail is your guests headshot. Category should be the top keyword you want to rank for on Itunes, and then tags/keywords lets you enter more. Then you use "Schedule Release" to say when it airs. You are almost done!

You have to get you podcast to iTunes because Libsyn has its own directory where people go and listen to podcasts. They are not as big; they're not iTunes. You have to tell them to put it on iTunes. So what you have to do is you take your RSS feed URL that Libsyn will give you (you go to destinations and hit view existing, and then copy the RSS feed) and you go paste it in iTunes here: Go to the iTunes podcast submission page at: https://phobos.apple.com/WebObjects/MZFinance.woa/wa/publishPodcast. Hit submit and then iTunes will notify you in a couple of days if they've accepted your podcast and then you will have a URL on iTunes, iTunes.com/whatever where your podcast is.

And every time you submit another episode, they're all on the same URL. You saw the original screenshot of my podcast with 40-some episodes, it's not a new website every time. It's your page on iTunes where they all will show up. And after you've done this once in iTunes, they accepted your podcast, you never have to do it again. Libsyn will automatically tell iTunes every week or every day or whenever you post an episode, they will automatically push it to iTunes and a couple of hours later it'll show up in the app store. Does that make sense? Yes.

How do you get them to come back for more? Because obviously you want people to keep listening to you. Think about it like you've got a radio station. You're having a conversation with the guest. You want to have your podcast be around a specific theme. Hopefully it's around what you're doing. I interviewed a guy who was a consumer podcaster. He's got now 10 different shows. He's created his own little network and they're each on a different topic. One is on technology. One's on lifestyle. One's on parenthood. So he's got a show with many episodes for each topic. You can have more than one podcast. But I would start with one. And you want to broadcast on a regular basis. I would say once a week, more if you want. It's up to you but at least once a week and on the same day every week. It's really important because you want to be predictable. You want people to know, oh it's Wednesday. I should go see if Seth posted a new episode. Instantly, I'm here on Wednesday. You want them tuning in. You got to think about it like it's a show on a radio station. If they never knew when it was going to show up, it would be really hard for them to listen to.

Again, it's more about the storytelling than anything else, and you're telling the story of your guest. My interviews go 15 minutes to half an hour. It all depends on the guest because I've a guest where I asked this question and I got a 10-second answer. The next week I asked a different guest the same question, I got half an hour and we didn't have time for anything else. You also have to get used to politely interrupting people because sometimes they will go on and on and on, and you need to stop them and either move on to the next question or cut them off, stop them to get them back on track because they will go off on tangents. You just get used to it, just say, "That's really great. You know what else I wanted to talk about was – Hey, you know, our listeners are asking me" – In the beginning, you may not have any listeners, but it's okay. They don't know that.

Our first listeners were me, myself and I. So the steps were: name your podcast. Again, we'll do the research to name it. Rate your introduction by a little bit about you, a little bit about the podcast, call to action. You're going to write your interview questions. Again, you can steal mine and just modify them. Get the Call Recorder app. Record your interview. Get your intro done or have us do it. Sign-up for Libsyn. Upload your first episode. Tell iTunes and repeat.

How do you turn it into a book is you transcribe the episode. You edit the episode and when you do enough of them, it turns into a book. So Cutting-Edge Marketing Magic was 15 interviews. With the e-mail you saw on HARO, of me interviewing other marketing people. Podcast Marketing Magic was me interviewing, I think it's 20 or 21 podcasters. And here's the really cool part is every single person – so after I hang up, the interview's over. I call him back. I say, "Wow, it was great. You obviously do this a lot. Thank you so much. Our listeners got so much out of that." They say, "Oh, thank you so much for having me. I really appreciate it." And so, you know, do you think it would make sense – would you be open to the idea of when the book comes out in May, you interviewing me on your podcast about you being in the book? Yeah, that would be great. I'd love to interview you about the fact that I was in the book.

So now, I'm getting interviewed on their podcast and they're promoting their podcast. So their podcast list or e-mail list, their social media saying, "Listen to the interview every week. Listen to the interview," and that's all linking to me. And of course, they're going to give me an opportunity on the show to talk – we're going to talk about the book. So we're going to say, I'm going to drop in several times throughout the interview. You know, if your listeners go to podcast marketingmagic.com or whatever the URL is that you got this from, I'm going to say, "They can get a copy of that book for only $4.95 shipping and handling." So I'm going to drop it in every couple, two to three times during the interview so that people go there.

So I now have all of these people who I interviewed promoting the fact that I did something with them. So Bill is interviewing home improvement people. They should buy a copy of the book for their sales people because they were in it. and then, of course, we should hire the guy that wrote a book about us and then you can do PR to your industry saying, "Look, home improvement contractor magazine, Bill Knoche just wrote a book." You should write about it. Here's a copy of the book. You should interview him and do a story on him. Does that makes sense?

You ask each guest to promote that they were on their show so they will promote, "Hey, you should tell your listeners that you were on my show." I'm going to promote to all my folks that I just interviewed you. You should promote to them, too. Of course, they should. Would you mind interviewing me on your show? Would you want to promote the fact that you are in a book. Of course, you do. It makes them look good.

I know I am giving you a lot of "how to" content in this chapter, but I wanted to make sure you got off to the right start.

Amazing Free Offer!

Register to attend a LIVE training session with me (Seth Greene), where I walk you through the same step-by-step process we use to get great results for our podcast and the podcast's of our clients.

You will Learn:

- How to Double Your Referrals with a Podcast!
- How to Get 20 Referral Partners Promoting Your Business in 20 Minutes A Week!
- How to Get Impossible To Reach Decision Makers To Seek You Out!

Go here to sign up, it's free:
http://www.ultimatemarketingmagician.com/pmmwebinar

I hope you got as much out of Market Domination for Podcasting as I did creating it!

Here are your next steps:

Register for the live training with me that is free to you as a reader of this book:

http://www.ultimatemarketingmagician.com/pmmwebinar

Subscribe to my top rated direct response marketing podcast for more great marketing ideas and interviews:

http://www.ultimatemarketingmagician.com/podcasts/

Remember the point of having a Podcast is not to have a podcast. Here are the points of having a Podcast:

1. With a Podcast you have a media platform. That means you are, in essence a reporter. Being a reporter who owns a media platform can get you access (as we will show you in later chapters) to people you otherwise couldn't get to, and places you couldn't otherwise go (can you say press pass?)

2. You are no longer chasing prospects or decision makers. You are now the person they seek out, as you have what everyone else wants – the ability to grant exposure (every business owner, thought leader, etc. wants more exposure).

3. You have something to promote every single week – your latest podcast episode.

4. You have a platform for repurposing content. Every episode of your podcast should be transcribed, edited, and turned into a chapter in your next book. That way you write a book without writing a book.

5. Guess who will promote your podcast? Everyone who appears on an episode! They were on it, so of course they will tell their email list and social media followers about it. Podcasting is a great way to get access to other people's lists – or build a list if you don't have one (or grow it really fast).

6. Guess who will promote your book? Everyone who is in it (your podcast guests)! So not only do they promote your podcast when their episode airs, but when the book comes out with them in it – they promote you all over again. It's a great way to create essentially an army of high level affiliates!

7. Let's take the example of one of our Done For You Podcasting clients, a financial advisor. If he asks an estate planning attorney to hand out his business card to all of the attorney's clients, that attorney will throw him out of his office. If our financial advisor puts the attorney on his podcast, and then in his book – our attorney will buy 200 copies of the book he is in, and happily hand them out to all his clients! Do you see how magical that is?

How would you like to be featured on my top rated podcast? Go here to apply to be interviewed:
http://www.ultimatemarketingmagician.com/podcast-guests/

And make sure you go check out this funny video I made you about everything that's wrong with marketing:
http://www.ultimatemarketingmagician.com/marketing-sucks

I look forward to hearing from you:

Seth Greene

A free eBook edition is available with the purchase of this book.

To claim your free eBook edition:

1. Download the Shelfie app.
2. Write your name in upper case in the box.
3. Use the Shelfie app to submit a photo.
4. Download your eBook to any device.

Shelfie

A free eBook edition is available
with the purchase of this print book.

CLEARLY PRINT YOUR NAME ABOVE IN UPPER CASE

Instructions to claim your free eBook edition:
1. Download the Shelfie app for Android or iOS
2. Write your name in **UPPER CASE** above
3. Use the Shelfie app to submit a photo
4. Download your eBook to any device

Print & Digital Together Forever.

Snap a photo

Free eBook

Read anywhere

The Morgan James Speakers Group

www.TheMorganJamesSpeakersGroup.com

We connect Morgan James published
authors with live and online events
and audiences whom will benefit
from their expertise.

Morgan James makes all of our titles available
through the Library for All Charity Organizations.

Printed in the USA
CPSIA information can be obtained
at www.ICGtesting.com
JSHW022215140824
68134JS00018B/1074